AN ISSUE WITH USSHER

The Doddridge Chronology

By Dennis D Doddridge

Knowest thou *not* this of old, since man was **placed** upon earth, *(Job 20:4; bold added)*

First edition, 30July2019
Second Edition, 09Mar2020

Updated 20Nov23 0619pm

An Issue with Ussher
Second Edition

ISBN: 9781711545455
B&W Edition
231120 0619

Published by DD Enterprises
PO Box 203, Allyn, WA 98524

Table of Contents

1. Introduction

The Bible is holy writ dating back thousands of years. It is generally believed that the prophet/scribe Moses was born between 1271BC and 1571BC. In ancient Hebraic script, he wrote or had the first five books of the Bible written down by scribes, as God dictated them. These books are known as the Five Books of Moses: Genesis, Exodus, Leviticus, Numbers and Deuteronomy.

Genesis begins with the organization of the earth, first spiritually then physically, to be inhabited by God's children. Starting with Adam and Eve, Moses provided enough detail about the earth's first 21 generations, to enable one to calculate a time span of more than 2,000 years. This is equal to 1/3 of the total mortal 6,000-year period that God planned should continue until the Millennium begins with the Second Coming of Christ.

The primary purpose of this mortal period is to prove the merits of God's spirit children, born to Him in "heaven" before the earth was to be inhabited by them. This testing will determine who among them shall be the rulers. The rest will be given other lesser eternal habitations. This trial was to be done without His immediate presence, so that we may exercise our "free will." It is to be for us as it was between the Philippians and Paul:

> That at the name of Jesus every knee should bow, of *things* in heaven, and *things* in earth, and *things* under the earth;

> And *that* every tongue should confess that Jesus Christ *is* Lord, to the glory of God the Father.
> Wherefore, my beloved, **as ye have always obeyed, not as in my presence only, but now much more in my absence,** work out your own salvation with fear and trembling. *(Philippians 2: 11, 12; ba)*

In fact, God foreknowing the severe testing was going to create world-wide failure, provided a Savior to compensate for their "sins" if they would repent of them and seek to do good works, enduring to the end.

> But with the precious blood of Christ, as of a lamb without blemish and without spot:
> **Who verily was foreordained before the foundation of the world,** but was manifest in these last times for you, *(1 Peter 1:19,20; ba)*

As Christ was fore-ordained (*before* the foundation of the world) to die for us, it makes sense that God also foreknew that the first immortal inhabitants placed on the earth, Adam and Eve, would also transgress the laws given to them.

Some believe erroneously that these two are doomed to hell for their transgression, because it brought mortality upon all of us. The truth is that *unless they failed*, we spirits would never have had the opportunity to come to this earth in the first place. Before the foundation of this world as spirits we were already born! And this was to be our next stop.

> 3 Blessed *be* the God and Father of our Lord Jesus Christ, who hath blessed us with all spiritual blessings in heavenly *places* in Christ:

> 4 According as he hath ***chosen us in him before the foundation of the world, that we should be*** holy and without blame before him in love:
>
> 5 Having predestinated us unto the adoption of children by Jesus Christ to himself, according to the good pleasure of his will, *(Eph 1:3-5; ba; predestinate = fore-ordain)*

"Should be" in verse 4 indicates it is not an irreversible act but using our agency *we are to become* holy and without blame by our efforts. Obedience is up to us.

Evidently then, God was not satisfied that we should go on in eternity as spirits without a mortal body, but with one made incorruptible and capable for an eternal existence.

> Now this I say, brethren, that flesh and blood cannot inherit the kingdom of God; neither doth corruption inherit incorruption.
>
> Behold, I shew you a mystery; We shall not all sleep, but we shall all be changed,
>
> In a moment, in the twinkling of an eye, at the last trump: for the trumpet shall sound, and the dead shall be raised incorruptible, and we shall be changed.
>
> For this corruptible must put on incorruption, and **this mortal *must* put on immortality.** *(1 Cor. 15:50-53; ba)*

So, the stage was set. A suitable earth was found for peopling from the gods starting with Adam and Eve.

> And thus a colony from heaven, it may be from the sun, is transplanted on our soil. *(PP Pratt, 1853, JR1,26:31)*

A spirit earth was first planned and created, then quietly integrated into it, a Garden of Eden was added, two immortal beings were put into the Garden, and a few laws were given to them thereby creating a measure of agency, to create conditions for failure. Further, opposition in the form of temptation by Lucifer was allowed. After an unknown amount of time, the dire effects of this scenario played out as anticipated by the Gods. Adam and Eve partook of a forbidden substance, breaking the law given them.

> 16 And the LORD God commanded the man, saying, Of every tree of the garden thou mayest freely eat:
> 17 But of the tree of the knowledge of good and evil, thou shalt not eat of it: for in the day that thou eatest thereof thou shalt surely die. *(Gen. 2:16,17)*

As a result, they fell and were removed from the Garden. They thereafter, and their offspring also, then spent their lives in a harsh mortal environment. This was the start of the 6,000-year mortal probationary plan period.

> ... This is the **plan of salvation** unto all men, through the blood of mine Only Begotten, who shall come in the meridian of time. *(Moses 6:62; ba)*
> 21 And the Gods prepared the waters that they might bring forth great whales, and every living creature that moveth, ... And the Gods saw that they would be obeyed, and that **their plan was good**. *(Abr. 4:21; ba)*

But where are we now in this probationary period? This is what Archbishop Ussher's work has led many to attempt to discover, resulting in an end-of-the-world melee in the year 2,000. But as well-intentioned as he was, there were some miscalculations. Hopefully, this book will correct some of the needed calculations to better establish the end of the world and how many years remain.

2. Archbishop Ussher

James Ussher was born 04Jan1581 in Dublin, Ireland of a prominent family.

In 1625, after progressing in the ranks in the Church of Ireland[1], an autonomous province of the Anglican Communion[2], he became the Archbishop of Armagh and gained the title as the Primate of All Ireland[3].

---

[1] "The Church of Ireland is a Christian church in Ireland and an autonomous province of the Anglican Communion."
(https://en.wikipedia.org/wiki/Church_of_Ireland,, May 2018)

[2] "The Communion is organised into a series of provinces and extra-provincial areas. The provinces are subdivided into dioceses, and the dioceses into parishes." *(https://www.anglicancommunion.org/structures/what-is-the-anglican-communion.aspx, May 2018)*

[3] "The Anglican Archbishop of Armagh is the ecclesiastical head of the Church of Ireland, bearing the title Primate of All Ireland," *(https://en.wikipedia.org/wiki/Archbishop_of_Armagh_(Church_of_Ireland), May 2018)*

He died 21Mar1656 at the age of 75. Among his many achievements and writings is a large book succinctly referred to as the Ussher Chronology, or the Annals of the World. Published in 1650, the full name is in Latin: *Annales Veteris Testamenti, a prima mundi origine deducti, una cum rerum Asiaticarum et Aegyptiacarum chronico, a temporis historici principio usque ad Maccabaicorum initia producto* ("Annals of the Old Testament, deduced from the first origins of the world, the chronicle of Asiatic and Egyptian matters together produced from the beginning of historical time up to the beginnings of Maccabees")[4].

He married Phoebe Challoner (1584-1654) in 1613. They had one child, a daughter they named Elizabeth (1619[20]-1693).

Citing numerous sources beyond merely the Holy Bible, Archbishop Ussher placed the beginning of time "4004BC ... happened at the start of the evening preceding the 23rd day of October in the year of the Julian calendar, 710" (see p. 104).

"The **Ussher chronology** is a 17th-century chronology of the history of the world formulated from a literal reading of the Old Testament by James Ussher .... The chronology is sometimes associated with young Earth creationism, which holds that the Universe was created only a few millennia ago by God ...." [5]

---

[4] Reference: *(https://en.wikipedia.org/wiki/Ussher_chronology, May 2018)*

[5] Reference: *(https://en.wikipedia.org/wiki/Ussher_chronology, May 2018)*

3. Scriptural Reliability

3a. Is the Bible Perfect?

Quick answer: no[6]. What? How can that be? Why should it be? Because God is perfect and therefore His scriptures must also be perfect, *isn't that the way it is*?

Here, many errors could be quoted to drive the point home illustrating the imperfections in the Bible. But just as many whitewashed errors could also be produced by zealots whose testimonies of the divinity of the Godhead hang by a thread on the idea the Scriptures must be perfect.

Most easily to illustrate are the many different versions of the Bible, and their many differences.

The Vulgate, The Martin Luther version, the King James version, St. Joseph Catholic edition, The Joseph Smith Translation and so on.

Then there are the many variations and contradictions within each of them.

Regarding the Book of Mormon, the prophet Nephi stated:

> Nevertheless, I do not write anything upon plates save it be that I think it be sacred. And now, if I do err, **even did they err of old;** not that I would excuse myself because of other men, but because of the weakness which is in me, according to the flesh, I would excuse myself. *(1 Ne. 19:6; ba)*

---

[6] However, see the conclusion of this chapter.

One of the Scriptures' thrust is to teach principles such as judgment, mercy, faith and charity. Its principles are perfect. Therefore, we may be sure that somehow or other, God will find a way to get His principles across to us.

> For verily I say unto you, Till heaven and earth pass, one jot or one tittle shall in no wise pass from the law, till all be fulfilled. *(Matt. 5:18; ddd: notice this verse refers to the Law of Moses, and not history lessons)*

How old somebody was when he died or how long Moses was in the desert, while adding possible interest to the stories, are in the end not eternal life saving. No one, I am sure we can safely purport, will be turned away from the highest heavens because they did not know the correct order of the five Books of Moses. If the scriptures mess up reporting less weighty information along with that which exalts, we must not get caught up in wresting such information to our decline.

> 15 And account *that* the longsuffering of our Lord *is* salvation; even as **our beloved brother Paul** also according to the wisdom given unto him hath written unto you;
> 16 As also in all *his* epistles, speaking in them of these things; **in which are some things hard to be understood**, which they that are unlearned and unstable wrest, as *they do* also the other scriptures, unto their own destruction. *(2 Pet 3:15, 16; ba)*

If God wants us to be saved, and the Scriptures were therefore perfect, why would He make anything in them "hard to be understood" for anyone?

Again, if the Scriptures were perfect, and they do tout the necessity of unity among His followers to be one with Him, then why aren't they clear enough so that there would not be any contrary and diverse positions, which have resulted in a myriad of different opinions and denominations of Christendom? Should God have hired a team of lawyers to write His books to make sure all ambiguities were removed? Joseph Smith relates:

> 8 During this time of great excitement my mind was called up to serious reflection and great uneasiness; but though my feelings were deep and often poignant, still I kept myself aloof from all these parties, though I attended their several meetings as often as occasion would permit. In process of time my mind became somewhat partial to the Methodist sect, and I felt some desire to be united with them; but so great were the confusion and strife among the different denominations, that it was impossible for a person young as I was, and so unacquainted with men and things, to come to any certain conclusion who was right and who was wrong.
>
> 9 My mind at times was greatly excited, the cry and tumult were so great and incessant. The Presbyterians were most decided against the Baptists and Methodists, and used all the powers of both reason and sophistry to prove their errors, or, at least, to make the people think they were in error. On the other hand, the Baptists and Methodists in their turn were equally zealous in endeavoring to establish their own tenets and disprove all others.
>
> 10 In the midst of this war of words and tumult of opinions, I often said to myself: What is to be done? Who of all these parties are right; or, are they all wrong together? If any one of them be right, which is it, and how shall I know it? *(JS-Hist 1:8-10)*

Obviously, the mere existence of a host of varying opposed Christian religions, each claiming their own views are the correct interpretation of true Biblical teachings, is proof in itself the Bible has failed to adequately reveal its doctrines clearly and perfectly.

> 15 And that from a child thou hast known the holy scriptures, which are able to make thee wise unto salvation through faith which is in Christ Jesus.
> 16 All scripture *is* given by inspiration of God, and *is* profitable for doctrine, for reproof, for correction, for instruction in righteousness:
> 17 That the man of God may be perfect, throughly furnished unto all good works. *(2 Tim. 3:15-17)*

Although God sends pure inspiration to a prophet; the prophet's (and/or that of a scribe's or a translator's) own bias and perception *may* slant the message accordingly. Hence, Paul might write, but it could be hard to understand, while Peter might have written the same message easy to understand.

> 23 Woe unto you, scribes and Pharisees, hypocrites! for ye pay tithe of mint and anise and cummin, and have omitted **the weightier *matters* of the law, judgment, mercy, and faith**: these ought ye to have done, and not to leave the other undone.
> *24 Ye* blind guides, which strain at a gnat, and swallow a camel. *(Matt. 23:23, 24; ba)*

The purported perfectness of the Bible has also produced nebulous conditions lending to the creation of blind guides straining at the Scriptures' gnats and swallowing a camel.

We might even correctly deduce that God has intentionally or at least knowingly left errors in the scriptures in order for us to recognize and concentrate our faith on the saving principles of the Scriptures, and let the scribes and Pharisees among us in sheep's clothing wrest the unimportant things to their own destruction.

While it is nice to try and calculate the chronology of the world, when it started and when it will end – after all, God did provide many clues how these events are to unfold in the end of times, yet correct understanding of this information will not be the determining factors which save us in the end. Orson Pratt spoke of the "mysteries" of the Scriptures.

> 9. Perhaps you may ask me why I dwell on this mysterious subject? I answer, why did the Lord dwell upon it forty-two years ago, if he did not want us **in some measure** to understand it? Would he speak at random? Would he give a revelation without expecting that the people would ever try to understand it?
>
> 10. If the Lord wished us to understand something, and condescended to reveal something, why should we, after forty-two years of experience, think that we are stepping over our bounds in **trying to approximately comprehend** what the Lord desired us to understand, in some measure, forty-two years ago?
>
> 11. It is an old sectarian whim and notion, to suppose that we must not **try to understand** revelation.
>
> 12. You know that when they come to something in the divine records which they do not understand, they will say – "Oh, the Lord never intended us to understand that, that is a mystery, we must not search into these things, they are mysteries."

13. Just as though the Lord would reveal something that he never intended or wished the human family to understand. Saying nothing about the Deity, it would be an act of foolishness on the part of a man to attempt a revelation of something that he never intended his fellow-men to understand.

14. The Lord is more consistent than man; and if he reveals anything, he surely intends that thing **to be for the profit and edification of the pure in heart**. *(Orson Pratt, Mar 14, 1875, JR1, 126:9-14; ba)*

Jesus spoke of His Second Coming.

42 **Watch therefore**: for ye know not what hour your Lord doth come.

43 But know this, that if the goodman of the house had known in what watch the thief would come, he would have watched, and would not have suffered his house to be broken up.

44 Therefore be ye also ready: for in such an hour as ye think not the Son of man cometh.

45 Who then is a faithful and wise servant, whom his lord hath made ruler over his household, to give them meat in due season?

46 Blessed *is* that servant, whom his lord when he cometh shall find so doing. *(Matt. 24:42-46; ba)*

The most important thing in the above scripture is not to figure out *when* exactly the Second Coming will happen, so we can *then* prepare ourselves, but rather to always be "so doing."

Ancient manuscripts.

Regarding our known sources of hard copies of the original manuscript scriptures, the following excerpts are quoted.

We now have discovered nearly 6,000 Greek manuscripts of the New Testament (NT). We don't know how many mistakes there are among our surviving copies, but they appear to number somewhere about 400,000. I will put this in comparative terms: there are far more differences in the NT manuscripts than there are words in the New Testament. *(https://outreachjudaism.org/400000-variants-in-the-nt-greek-manuscript/, viewed: Jun2019.)*

None of the original documents of the New Testament is known to scholars to be extant; and the existing manuscripts differ from one another. ...
Every year, several New Testament manuscripts handwritten in the original Greek format are discovered. The latest substantial find was in 2008, when 47 new manuscripts were discovered in Albania; at least 17 of them unknown to Western scholars. When comparing one manuscript to another, with the exception of the smallest fragments, no two copies agree completely throughout. There has been an estimate of 400,000 variations among all these manuscripts (from the 2nd to 15th century) which is more than there are words in the New Testament. *(https://en.wikipedia.org/wiki/Biblical_manuscript, viewed 02Jun2015).*

The scriptures were put together by authorities of religions anciently. Some Scriptures included the Apocrypha, others left them out. There are a number of times in our scriptures where certain books are referred to by the ancient writers and prophets, but those inspired writings are non-existent in our package of books called the Bible. Quite a few of the books in the Bible do not have a known author, and we are left to wonder whether the monks and assemblers long ago did right by including them or not.

Paul mentions a few times that what he was about to say was not inspired by God, but rather he was going to give his own opinion[7]. How many others likewise gave their own opinions about a matter, but did not bother to pre-state them by elucidating that fact?

> 39 Search the scriptures; for in them ye think ye have eternal life: and they are they which testify of me.
> 40 And **ye will not come to me**, that ye might have life. *(John 5:39, 40; ba)*

Notice Jesus says that *for those who will not come unto Him for eternal life* to go ahead and spend their time searching the scriptures looking for it. While He says they do in fact testify of him, it is not the Scriptures per se that have eternal life, but rather *the act* of coming to Him that provides eternal life. Searching is a process, not the end.

Also, consider that if we are to *search* a book for something then it is equally clear the *entire* book does not contain what it is we are looking for, but only something *in* it – otherwise, why are we leafing through the many pages of the book *searching* for the something we are trying to find, and passing up that which is not what we are searching for?

The Bible and the prophets are *aids* to help us and guide us toward the goal of finding what it is what we need to be *doing* in order for us to be united and one with God.

---

[7] Example: 1 Cor. 7:12: [Paul] But to the rest speak I, **not the Lord**: If any brother hath a wife that believeth not, and she be pleased to dwell with him, let him not put her away. *(ba)*

Surely the Lord GOD will do nothing, but he revealeth his secret unto his servants the prophets. *(Amos 3:7)*

But the perfection we seek is not necessarily the book itself, but rather what the book conveys as a whole. It is in our hearts, our minds, and our faith, hope, works and actions that ultimately will unite us with His grace for eternity. Without inspiration and revelation, we are as ships without rudders.

Where *there is* no vision, the people perish: but he that keepeth the law, happy *is* he *(Prov. 29:18; The Martin Luther version:* Wo keine Weissagung ist, wird das Volk wild und wüst; wohl aber dem, der das Gesetz handhabet! Translated: Where [there] is no prophecy, the people become wild and confused; it is however well with them who implement the law).

11 And he gave some, apostles; and some, prophets; and some, evangelists; and some, pastors and teachers;

12 For the perfecting of the saints, for the work of the ministry, for the edifying of the body of Christ:

13 Till we all come in **the unity of the faith**, and of the knowledge of the Son of God, **unto a perfect man**, unto the measure of the stature of the fulness of Christ:

14 That we *henceforth* be no more children, tossed to and fro, and carried about with every wind of doctrine, by the sleight of men, *and* cunning craftiness, whereby they lie in wait to deceive;

15 But speaking the truth in love, may grow up into him in all things, which is the head, *even* Christ: *(Eph. 4:11-15; ba)*

Thus, we find "the perfect man" not in searching the Scriptures only, but in the act of *coming* unto Christ, as taught and encouraged *by the prophets and apostles, etc.* Their work is to perfect us. Are we all now in the unity of the faith? Not even close. Hence, these apostles and prophets, teachers, pastors and evangelists, etc. are still needed today.

Searching and Doing

22 But **be ye doers of the word, and not hearers only**, deceiving your own selves.

23 For if any be a hearer of the word, and not a doer, he is like unto a man beholding his natural face in a glass:

24 For he beholdeth himself, and goeth his way, and straightway forgetteth what manner of man he was.

25 But whoso looketh into the perfect law of liberty, and continueth *therein,* he being not a forgetful hearer, but a doer of the work, this man shall be blessed in his deed.

26 If any man among you seem to be religious, and bridleth not his tongue, but deceiveth his own heart, this man's religion *is* vain.

27 Pure religion and undefiled before God and the Father is this, To visit the fatherless and widows in their affliction, *and* to keep himself unspotted from the world. *(James 1:22-27; ba)*

Reading and searching are vital to learn what we are to do. But if we do not heed personal inspiration and "come unto Christ" and keep his commandments and perform His works, our religion is in vain.

How then shall they call on him in whom they have not believed? and how shall they believe in him of whom they have not heard? and how shall they hear without a preacher? *(Rom. 10:14)*

God *allows* errors in the Scriptures. But He gives us correct understanding by personal inspiration and revelation. To those who refuse inspiration and revelation, the errors may become stumbling blocks.

> 7 What then? Israel hath not obtained that which he seeketh for; but the election hath obtained it, and the rest were blinded
> 8 (According as it is written, God hath given them the spirit of slumber, eyes that they should not see, and ears that they should not hear;) unto this day.
> 9 And David saith, Let their table be made a snare, and a trap, and **a stumbling block**, and a recompence unto them:
> 10 Let their eyes be darkened, that they may not see, and bow down their back alway.
> 11 I say then, Have they stumbled that they should fall? God forbid: but *rather* through their fall salvation *is come* unto the Gentiles, for to provoke them to jealousy. *(Rom. 11:7-11; ba)*

Those that are of the obedient elect of God have obtained what they have sought, whereas the rest were blinded. The rest have tripped on stumbling blocks. Finding fault with the imperfections of the Scriptures is a stumbling block. Demanding scriptural perfection as a condition of their faith is a stumbling block. The perfection we should seek is through active faith and obedience – being doers of the word; hearing and reading being the instruments to lead us there.

> For **we labor diligently to write**, to persuade our children, and also our brethren, **to believe in Christ**, and **to be reconciled to God**; for we know that **it is by grace that we are saved, after all we can do.** *(2 Ne. 25:23; ba)*

4. The Issue

If we can trace our own individual genealogy back far enough, we discover that we are all related at some point with each other, and that all of mankind has a single ancestor – Adam. The Bible provides the same for Jesus Christ. Starting with Jesus, the Bible provides a list of his fathers all the way back to Adam, encompassing 60 generations in all. The most ancient of these fathers had extra-ordinarily long lives such as 930 years of age for Adam, 969 years for Methuselah, and 950 years for Noah. The first nine (Adam to Noah less Enoch) of these patriarchs lived an average of about 912 years. But as time went on the average life span trend of these Patriarchs, decreased to the mid-100s, and then finally down to 120 years or less.

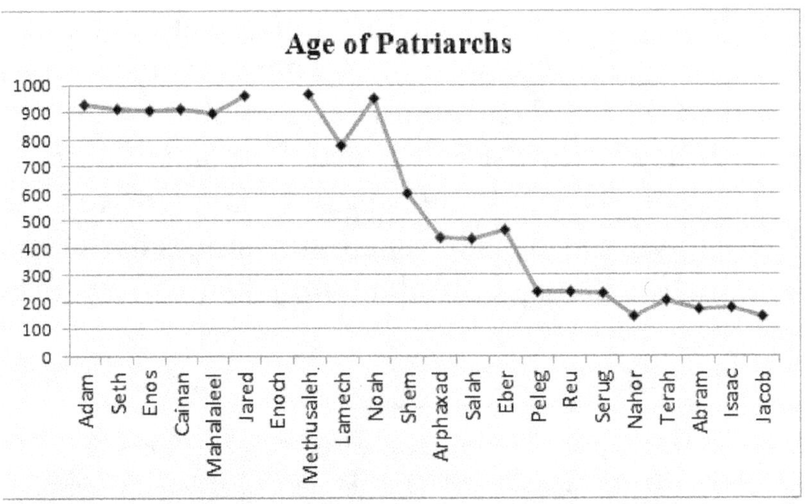

By faith Enoch was translated that he should not see death; and was not found, because God had translated him... (Heb. 11:5)

> And the LORD said, My spirit shall not always strive with man, for that he also *is* flesh: **yet his days shall be an hundred and twenty years**. *(Gen. 6:3; ba)*

Concomitantly, the earliest Patriarchs did not beget their firstborn sons (lineage was Patriarchal) until they were at least a century old, or close to it. This meant that within 21 generations 2,098 years[8] had passed away since Adam stepped out of the Garden of Eden.

Christ was born in 5BC, according to Ussher, or 1AD per Doddridge. The question then bursts out: of the remaining 38 generations between Jacob and the birth of Jesus (60-21 = 39 – Jesus (no son) = 38), how many years passed away? If we can determine that, then we can arrive at the year Adam entered mortality. To know that, we need to know the *birth-age*[9] of each of those 38 fathers when he begat the next son in the line of descent. Unfortunately, the Bible does not give us this information. We know that Isaac was not able to have his direct line of descent son Jacob until he was 60 years old. And Abraham, due to being tested by God, did not have his son Isaac until he was 100 years old. And Terah, a polytheist, because of circumstances in the land of Ur, did not beget Abraham until he was 70 years old.[10]

---

[8] KJV=2106 years, Ussher = 2168 years, JST = 2098 years.

[9] *Age of father when he had his hierarchal or firstborn son – herein referred to as "birth-age" or "birth-year."*

[10] Ussher purports Terah's birth-age of 130. See p.115. *ddd note: if that were true why was Abraham so surprised for his own late procreating?*

4a. The Meridian of Time

> 45...When shall the blood of the Righteous be shed, that all they that mourn may be sanctified and have eternal life?
> 46 And the Lord said: **It shall be in the meridian of time,** in the days of wickedness and vengeance. *(Moses 7:45,46)*

The locution, "in the meridian of time," is found but six times[11] in scripture, all unique to scripture from the Restored Church. Five of these six refer to the *coming* of Christ, i.e., His birth; the sixth refers to His sacrifice at the *end* of His life in mortality.

In the first edition of this book, I originally considered the Meridian of Time in context with *this* earth, that it was a specific date – the halfway point in our 7,000-year temporal existence. While that half-way point certainly is the case, perhaps we should consider using God's time as reckoned per Kolob[12] for the Meridian of Time about the pre-mortal mission of Jesus Christ. Notice the verse above does *not* say **at** the meridian of time but rather **in** it. The meridian of time is a *period of time,*

---

[11] D&C 20:26; 39:3; Moses 5:57; 6:57; 6:62; 7:46.

[12] 3 And the Lord said unto me: These are the governing ones; and the name of the great one is Kolob, because it is near unto me, for I am the Lord thy God: **I have set this one to govern all those which belong to the same order** as that upon which thou standest.
4 And the Lord said unto me, by the Urim and Thummim, that Kolob was after the manner of the Lord, according to its times and seasons in the revolutions thereof; that one revolution was a day unto the Lord, after his manner of reckoning, it being one thousand years according to the time appointed unto that whereon thou standest. This is the reckoning of the Lord's time, according to the reckoning of Kolob. *(Abr. 3:3,4; ba)*

not necessarily a specific 24-hour day or a 365-day year in the earth's calendars.

Terms.

- *Millennium* is defined as a 1,000-year period.
- Older dictionary definitions of **Meridian** suggest the center or high point (of a development).
- Within the context of this chapter's scriptural narrative, *day* is defined as one Kolob day, equaling 1,000 earth years.
- Within the context of this chapter's scriptural narrative, *time* is defined as one Kolob day, equaling 1,000 earth years. It can also refer to the entire 7,000-year Temporal Existence.

But, beloved, be not ignorant of this one thing, that one day *is* with the Lord as a thousand years, and a thousand years as one day. *(2 Pet.3:8)*

1 Fig. 1.   Kolob, signifying the first creation, nearest to the celestial, or the residence of God.   First in government, the last pertaining to the measurement of time. The measurement according to celestial time, which **celestial time** signifies one day to a cubit. One day in Kolob is equal to a thousand years according to the measurement of this earth, which is called by the Egyptians Jah-oh-eh. *(Abr. 2 Facsimile)*

But of the tree of knowledge of good and evil, thou shalt not eat of it; for in the time that thou eatest thereof, thou shalt surely die. Now I, Abraham, saw that it was after **the Lord's time**, which was after the time of Kolob; **for as yet** the Gods had not appointed unto Adam his reckoning. *(Abr. 5:13; ba)*

At some point God set "unto Adam his reckoning," that is, reckoning after our earth's revolutions. But the Meridian of Time reckoning was set in our premortal state, not afterwards.

The term *Meridian of time* may be defined as the *high point* of the *seven one thousand-year periods*. As the earth is destined to experience a 7,000-year

Temporal Existence, the *Meridian of time* comprises the middle point of that existence. In other words, it is the center of the Temporal Existence, the 4th thousand-year period. Just as Adam was told he would die **in** the *day* he partook of the fruit (yet it was not until near the end of that 1,000-year day) we should expect Christ's birth to be sometime **in** the 4th period of time, the meridian 1,000-year day.

> But of the tree of the knowledge of good and evil, thou shalt not eat of it: for **in the day** that thou eatest thereof thou shalt surely die. *(Gen. 2:17)*

Time.

Noteworthy is the use of the term *time* in the fourth and fifth chapters of the Book of Abraham:

> 4:1 [the Gods, organized and formed the heavens and the earth.
> And they (the Gods) said: Let there be light; and there was light]
> 4:8 [the expanse] and this was the **second time** that they called night and day.
> 13 [the Gods pronounced the dry land, Earth] the **third time.**
> 19 [the Gods organized the two great lights] it was the **fourth time**.
> 23 [great whales, and every living creature that moveth, which the waters were to bring forth ... after their kind; and every winged fowl after their kind] it was the **fifth time.**
> 31 [great whales, and every living creature that moveth, which the waters were to bring forth abundantly after their kind; and every winged fowl after their kind] and they numbered the **sixth time.**
> 5:3 [on the **seventh time** they would rest from all their works which they (the Gods) counseled among themselves to form; and sanctified it] the Gods

concluded upon the seventh time, ... (Abr chapters 4&5; ddd note: the "first time" is not named as such. Each of these times equals 1,000 years.)

In the Book of Genesis and also in the Book of Moses, both written by Moses, these *times* are simply referred to as "days." And as it was quoted earlier, Adam was to die "for **in the day** that thou eatest thereof thou shalt surely die" day signifying a 1,000-year period. But Abraham's writings add an element of detail not found in Moses' writings: creation days are also known as "times." And since we know that in the case of Adam, "day" means a 1,000-year Kolob day, then in the seven *times* mentioned by Abraham, we are speaking of seven one thousand year periods of creation.

The "second time," "third time," etc. are each 1,000 year periods, hence, the creation of the earth comprises 6,000 years mostly of *counseling, planning and organizing* to do what would actually be physically accomplished later in the single last 1,000 year period of time in the creation, the seventh time. And in the seventh time, everything was thereafter sanctified.

Orson Pratt has explained this subject of creation many times. Here I quote from his The Seer[13].

---

[13] It should be noted that Elder Orson Pratt in the Seer and in several of his other publications deliberated on various subjects, and many of his conclusions were quite at odds with the presiding president of the Church at that time, namely, Brigham Young. His last sentence in the excerpt here, in my estimation, can only be correct if we are not considering that which was produced by evolution. To my knowledge, Orson Pratt did not accept evolution.

55. As the tabernacle of Adam was formed out of the dust on the seventh day, so were the tabernacles of every species of animals, birds, and fish, together with every variety of vegetables, all formed on the seventh day. This idea is clearly revealed in Joseph Smith's inspired translation of the second chapter of Genesis*, from which we have already made an extract in the 18th paragraph; by reference to which it will be seen that Man was "the first flesh upon the earth, the first Man also," and as he was made on the seventh day or period, all the rest must have been made on the seventh. The garden was planted on the seventh, and Man was placed in the garden on the seventh. Every beast and fowl was made out of the ground and brought to Adam to be named on the seventh day. Eve also was made out of one of his ribs on the seventh day. All the grass, and herbs, and trees. according to their kinds, were made to grow out of the ground on the seventh day or time. And before the seventh day there was no vegetable or animal existence on our earth. *(The Seer, pp.68, 69)*

* 8. And I, the Lord God, formed man from the dust of the ground, and breathed into his nostrils the breath of life; and man became a living soul, the first flesh upon the earth, the first man also;

9. Nevertheless, all things were before created, but spiritually were they created and made, according to my word. *(Gen.2:8,9 JST)*

There are then two 7,000-year periods explained in Scripture. They total 14,000 years – the first period is *spiritual creation*, followed by the second period of the *natural creation*.

... We are to understand that as God made the world in six days, and on the seventh day he finished his work, and sanctified it, and also formed man out of the dust of the earth, even so, in the beginning of the seventh thousand years will the Lord God sanctify the earth, and complete the salvation of man, and judge all things, and shall redeem all things, except that which he hath not put into his power, when he shall have sealed all things, unto the end of all things; and the sounding of the trumpets of the seven angels are the preparing and finishing of his work, in the beginning of the seventh thousand years—the preparing of the way before the time of his coming. *(D&C 77:12)*

In toto, the *spiritual creation* comprised the forming, planning, counselling, and introduction of spiritual life, onto this earth which had been previously void of organized *spirit* life.

And the earth was without form, and void; ... *(Gen.1:4 JST)*

The second period of seven millennia (7,000 years), *the natural or "physical" creation,* is presently actively engaged in carrying out all of which was originally performed and placed into motion in the first period and will culminate in its sanctification and redemption during the forthcoming Millennium.

4 Where wast thou when I laid the foundations of the earth? declare, if thou hast understanding.
5 Who hath laid the measures thereof, if thou knowest? or who hath stretched the line upon it?
6 Whereupon are the foundations thereof fastened? or who laid the corner stone thereof;
7 When the morning stars sang together, and all the sons of God shouted for joy? *(Job 38:4-7. Ddd note:* Job, of course, had no recollection of his pre-mortal existence, and that *he,* as well as *we,* were in fact, those *"morning stars"* that sang together.*)*

4b. The Arphaxad-Nahor Seven.

Seven generations are cited in the Scriptures, from Arphaxad, the son of Shem, through Nahor the father of Terah with a new commonality. These are the first who had what we might deem as having their birth-year at a more normal age, between 35 and 29, *averaging 31.4* for the seven. For the Arphaxad-Nahor Seven there was no known stressful situation recorded or testing by God that might cause them to postpone having their firstborn sons, though the Book of Abraham records a famine in the days of Terah, the son of Nahor. Further, the longevity of these seven fathers had been cut in half or more, from 438 years by Arphaxad down to 148 for Nahor.

If the last 38 generations, from Judas to Jesus, had gotten back to the scripturally shown normal 31.4 average birth-age, then only 1,193 years (38 x 31.4 = 1,193) would have passed away. This means we could *by use of an unadjusted averaging* determine Adam's "birth" to be at 3291BC (1,193 years + 2,098* years = 3,291). Yet Ussher says it was in 4004BC, or 713 years more than what employing an unadjusted averaging would dictate for those 38 fathers (4004 – 3291 = 713). Doddridge would be 449 years more (**3740-3291 = 449).   *see p.22; **see next page; p.83.

Now, there were a few exceptions indeed during the span of the 38 generations that would warrant raising the birth-age average somewhat over the Arphaxad-Nahor Seven. And we will assess them in this book.

The main issue in this book is that Ussher's chronology, if we instead implement more justifiable averages for the unknowns, he comes up rather high in comparison, particularly due to adding on 264 years to the earth's mortal history, over that of Doddridge (4004-3740 = 264).

On the other hand, the Doddridge chronology, after considering numerous varying scenarios and employing the Arphaxad-Nahor Seven 31.4-year average as its base point, and reviewing other credible studies, as well as integrating the wars and general tumult of the Israelis during that time, finally culminated its research with 37.85-year averages (see p.67). This resulted in a **3740BC** starting point, instead of Ussher's 4004BC. With what amounts to be a 66-year average from Judah to Jesse for Ussher, Doddridge splits up the same period using 37.85 and 59 respectively, or a 49.7-year average overall.

Therefore, this book wishes to address Ussher's deviation from Biblical trends in averages, if he ever used them at all, covering unknown portions in the Biblical patriarchal descendancy – in particular, the diminishing ages of father's having their firstborn sons. The result of considering established averages to cover unknown birth-ages will show a quantitative variance between Ussher's dating of our genealogy to what should be a more realistic one.

In conclusion of this discussion, moving down the Biblical father-firstborn son genealogy, the Bible provides the needed information of only the first 21 patriarchs, i.e., the ages of the fathers when they had their firstborn sons. Beginning with Jacob, the 22nd in the line of descendancy from Adam and on to Jesus Christ the 60th in the line, much supplemental data is generally provided: ages at death, who begat who and so on, are stated, but *not* the critically needed age of the father when he had his firstborn son.

The question naturally arises "Why do we need to know the age of the father when he had his firstborn son?" The objective of this book is to provide a possibly more accurate estimation of when this world began, or rather, when the "man" Adam was first *placed* on this earth,

> Knowest thou *not* this of old, since man was **placed** upon earth, *(Job 20:4; ba),*

then vacating Eden, and then to structure the successive genealogies down to Jesus Christ. From there we can add, approximately, the remaining number of years until the end of the world and then establish a possible approximation for the Second Coming and the Millennium.

Yes, we *can* get a fair idea of the full span, though,

> 35 Heaven and earth shall pass away, but my words shall not pass away.
> 36 But of that **day and hour** knoweth no *man,* no, not the angels of heaven, but my Father only. *(Matt. 24:35, 36; ba)*

Note, that while we cannot establish *the day and the hour*, we might get to the nearest century. If Ussher was right, he setting Adams' departure from the

Garden at the 23rd day of October, 4004BC, then we might deduce the day of the Second coming as the 23rd day of October, 1996AD (4,004+1,996=6,000) less a period for the unknown "days" being shortened to save the elect. Well, that day has come and gone. Another issue with Ussher. But then I do not think in 1650 he was thinking in terms of a 6,000-year period for mortality. But maybe he was, as 1996AD was still over 300 years into the future for him.

6,000 years mortal existence

-

4,004 BC

=

1,996 to the end of the mortal existence (the year 1996 has come and gone)

-

A period of time for the "days shortened" *(Matt. 24:22)*

=

The time of the Second coming.

It is now at this writing, the year 2020. Thus, the *days shortened* are at least (2020-1996=) 24 years overextended. The Ussher Chronology (if the 4004BC figure had been correct) has missed the Second Coming by 24 years at least so far.

4c. Israel's Affliction in Egypt

In addition to the earth's temporal existence chronology, the scriptures describe certain contiguous periods of time for particular episodes of Biblical history. Two of them are (1) Israel's affliction, and (2) the Exodus from Egypt. Therefore, it might prove advantageous to review them, and weigh their merit and possible effect, relevancy and accuracy to the overall chronology.

One double check for calculating the earth's chronology after the gods began populating it with their spirit children into mortality, is the subject of Israel's migration into Egypt, their subsequent enslavement, and their Exodus back to the Promised Land. This covers the time that Abram was promised his seed would possess Israel but only after a 400+ year period of time to be spent in servitude in exile, in the land of Egypt, until their return to the land of milk and honey and freedom.

Including this part of history and inserting it into the chronology being evaluated may lead to improved averaging calculations in the overall chronological span, tweaking the averages as necessary.

When did the Affliction start?

Some have speculated the 430-year period of affliction began with the arrival of Abraham in Canaan, rather than the death of Joseph, to start the prophecy. This viewpoint would certainly add in sufficient years to the whole sum to build the case for a four-plus century figure.

However, the 430-year prophecy emphasizes it should begin when "**thy** [Abraham's] **seed** shall be a stranger **in a land** *that is* **not theirs**; ..." *(Gen. 15:13; ba)*. Furthermore, the prophecy states that Canaan was given to Abraham by covenant as his property "**In the same day**" *(Gen. 17:8; ba)*. Therefore, going to Canaan could not be going to a land that is not theirs as Canaan was now a land that "is" theirs. It should be evident then that the prophecy did not start with Abraham going to his land of Canaan.

When did Abraham's seed become a stranger in a land that was not theirs? Answer: after Joseph died, he and all of his generation, and the new Pharaoh began to rule and to afflict Jacob's progeny.

> 6 And Joseph died, and all his brethren, and all that generation.
> 7 And the children of Israel were fruitful, and increased abundantly, and multiplied, and waxed exceeding mighty; and the land was filled with them.
> 8 Now there arose up a new king over Egypt, which knew not Joseph.
> 9 And he said unto his people, Behold, the people of the children of Israel *are* more and mightier than we:
> 10 Come on, let us deal wisely with them; lest they multiply, and it come to pass, that, when there falleth out any war, they join also unto our enemies, and fight against us, and *so* get them up out of the land.
> 11 Therefore they did set over them taskmasters **to afflict them** with their burdens. *(Exo. 1:6-11; ba)*

When did this happen? The Scriptures do not provide us with an exact time, but the narration of events leading up to the time do give us a possible approximation.

By working backwards (and jumping around), we can calculate an approximate time when Judah and Joseph were born. Judah's birth year is of value to better estimate the timeline between Adam and Jesus. Joseph's birth (and death) is of value to better estimate the timeline of the Abraham "affliction" prophecy.

First, we are given certain facts.

1) Before Jacob came to Egypt, Joseph was there. Joseph was thirty years old when he met the Pharaoh and explained Pharaoh's dream.

> And **Joseph *was* thirty years old** when he stood before Pharaoh king of Egypt. *(Gen. 41:46)*

2) Seven years of plenty transpire.

> And in the seven plenteous years the earth brought forth by handfuls. *(Gen. 41:47; now **Joseph was 37***)*

3) Two years into the seven-year famine transpire, and Joseph reunites with his brothers. **Joseph: age 39**. The second year of the famine was after the seven years of plenty. As Joseph explained to his brothers:

> 6 For these two years *hath* the famine *been* in the land: and yet *there are* five years, ... 13 And ye shall tell my father of all my glory in Egypt, and of all that ye have seen: and ye shall haste and bring down my father hither. *(Gen. 45:6, 13)*

4) Brothers hastily retrieve Jacob and Jacob reunites with Joseph in Egypt (age 39).

5) Pharaoh meets Jacob and asks how old he was. Jacob: age 130. 130 minus 39 = 91. Jacob was 130 years old when he

came to Egypt in the second year of the famine. Jacob was 130 years old when Joseph was 39. Therefore, Jacob was 91 when Joseph was born.

> 8 And Pharaoh said unto Jacob, How old *art* thou?
> 9 And Jacob said unto Pharaoh, The days of the years of my pilgrimage *are* an hundred and thirty years: ... *(Gen. 47:8,9)*

6) Joseph's birth then would have been *about* 1551BC if Adam left the Garden in 3740BC.

7) This would also mean that Judah [Judas] would have been born in *about* -1559BC, about eight years before Joseph.

8) Jacob was 147 years old when he died. The last 17 years of his life was in Egypt

> And Jacob lived in the land of Egypt seventeen years: so the whole age of Jacob was an hundred forty and seven years. *(Gen.47:28; 147 – 17 = 130)*

Determining Birth-Years of Judah and Joseph, Part I

Year	Event	Reference
-1702	**Isaac Born**	Gen. 21:5
-1662	Isaac (age 40) marries Rebekah	Gen. 24:67; 25:20
-1642	**Isaac (age 60) has** Esau and **Jacob**	Gen. 26:26
-1563	Jacob marries (age 79) Leah and Rachel	Gen. 29:16-30
-1563	Leah pregnant with Reuben	Gen. 29:31
-1562	Leah begets Reuben	Gen. 29:32
-1561	Leah begets Simeon	Gen. 29:33
-1560	Leah begets Levi	Gen. 29:34
-1559	**Leah begets Judah**	Gen. 29:35
-1558	Bilhah begets Dan	Gen. 30:6
-1557	Bilhah begets Nephtali	Gen. 30:8
-1556	Zilpah begets Gad	Gen. 30:11
-1555	Zilpah begets Asher	Gen. 30:13
-1554	Leah begets Issachar	Gen. 30:18
-1553	Leah begets Zebulun	Gen. 30:20
-1552	Leah begets Dinah	Gen. 30:21
-1551	**Rachel begets Joseph**	Gen. 30:24

Determining Birth-Years of Judah and Joseph, Part II

Line	Event	Years	Year	Reference	Quote
1	Age of Isaac when he had Jacob / Esau	60	-1642	Gen. 25:26	...Jacob: and Isaac was threescore years old when she bare them.
2	Age of Joseph when he meets Pharaoh first time	**30**	-1612	Gen. 41:46	And Joseph was thirty years old when he stood before Pharaoh king of Egypt.
3	Years of plenty	**7**	-1605	Gen. 41:53	And the seven years of plenteousness, that was in the land of Egypt, were ended.
4	Two years of famine to drive Jacob into Egypt	**2**	-1603	Gen. 45:6	For these two years hath the famine been in the land: and yet there are five years,
5	Age of Joseph when Jacob meets Pharaoh	**39**	-1603		Add lines 2,3,4.
6	Age of Jacob when he meets Pharaoh	130	-1603	Gen. 47:9	And Jacob said unto Pharaoh, The days of the years of my pilgrimage are an hundred and thirty years
7	Minus line 5	(39)			Used to calculate line 8.
8	Age of Jacob when he had Joseph	91	-1551		Subtract Line 5 from line 6
9	Age of Jacob when he married Leah & Rachel	79	-1563		Line 8 - 12 years (Joseph was last of 12 children all born over an est. 12 years).
10	Age of Jacob when he started working for Laban	72	-1570	Gen. 29:20	And Jacob served seven years for Rachel. (Line 9 – 7 years)
11	Age of Jacob when Isaac died	120	-1522	Gen. 35:28	And the days of Isaac were an hundred and fourscore years. (180 -Line 1[60]).
12	Age of Jacob when he had Judah	83	-1559		About 8 years before Joseph. Judah was the 4th, Joseph was the 12th. (See Line 8 less 8 years; Gen.29:28 thru 30:24).
13	Age of Joseph when he died	110	-1441	Gen. 50:22	So Joseph died, *being* an hundred and ten years old ...
14	Age of Judah when he died	119	-1440		Age per the 1906 Jewish Encyclopedia. See Jewishencyclopedia.com *(viewed 02Apr20)*
15	Onset of the Affliction		-1440	Exo. 1:6-11	6 And Joseph died, and all his brethren, and all that generation. ... 8 Now there arose up a new king over Egypt, which knew not Joseph. ... 11 Therefore they did set over them taskmasters **to afflict them with their burdens.** ... *(ba)*

How long will the affliction last?

Let's consider certain scriptures, starting with Abraham's prophecy.

(1)
400 years

Gen.15:12 And when the sun was going down, a deep sleep fell upon Abram; and, lo, an horror of great darkness fell upon him.

13 And he said unto Abram, Know of a surety that **thy seed shall be a stranger in a land** *that is* **not theirs, and shall serve them; and they shall afflict them four hundred years**[14];

14 And also that nation, whom they shall serve, will I judge: **and afterward shall they come out with great substance**[15].

15 And thou shalt go to thy fathers in peace; thou shalt be buried in a good old age.

16 But **in the fourth generation** they shall come hither again: for the iniquity of the Amorites *is* not yet full.

17 And it came to pass, that, when the sun went down, and it was dark, behold a smoking furnace, and a burning lamp that passed between those pieces.

---

[14] Verse 13. Note that "a land" indicates a singular location that is *not theirs* which was the land of Canaan and other neighboring areas, and which was designated theirs on the "same day" (v18). Hence the *serving* did not occur in Canaan or anywhere in the land of Israel (v18-21; 17:8).

[15] Verses 13,14. Notice the use of the word "serve" as opposed to "affliction." The question arises, does the *serving* overlap the period of time of *affliction*? In other words, could the *serving* in a land that is not theirs begin before the *affliction* started, but the *affliction* of it continue beyond the period of time of *serving* – i.e., the *affliction* was to be about 172 years, but the *serving* and the *affliction* together purportedly total 400 years? Verse 13 does use the word "and" to separate the two actions.

18 In the same day the LORD made a covenant with Abram, saying, Unto thy seed have I given this land, from the river of Egypt unto the great river, the river Euphrates:
19 The Kenites, and the Kenizzites, and the Kadmonites,
20 And the Hittites, and the Perizzites, and the Rephaims,
21 And the Amorites, and the Canaanites, and the Girgashites, and the Jebusites.
17:8 And I will give unto thee, and to thy seed after thee, the land wherein thou art a stranger, all the land of Canaan, for an everlasting possession; and I will be their God. *(Gen. 15:12-21, 17:8; ba)*

Verse 13: who are "they?" The Egyptians. Verses 13 and 14, broken down into bullets we have:

1) "Thy seed shall be a stranger **in a land *that is* not theirs,**
2) and **shall serve them**
3) and **they shall afflict them four hundred years**
4) and **afterward shall they come out also [from] that nation, whom they served** ....

We also learn what the land of Israel should consist of, namely from the river of Egypt unto the River Euphrates. Thus, so long as the seed of Israel were in that land, they were in *their* own land – and not as strangers in the land wherein they would be serving foreign masters. Not until they left their own land could the purported 400-year prophecy begin.

(2)

430 years

40 Now the sojourning of the **children of Israel, who dwelt in Egypt,** *was* **four hundred and thirty years.**[16]
41 And it came to pass **at the end of the four hundred and thirty years, even the selfsame day** it came to pass, that all the hosts of the LORD went out from the land of Egypt. *(Exo. 12:40,41; ba)*

(3)

430 years

And this I say, *that* **the covenant**, that was confirmed before of God in Christ, **the law, which was four hundred and thirty years after**, cannot disannul, that it should make the promise of none effect. *(Gal. 3:17; ba)*[17]

In Martin Luther German version [MLV] (for possible clarification):

Ich meine aber dies: Das Testament, das von Gott zuvor bestätigt ist, wird nicht aufgehoben durch das Gesetz, welches vierhundertdreißig Jahre hernach gegeben ist, so daß die Verheißung zunichte wurde.

Translation:

I mean however this: The Testament, that God previously confirmed, will not be abolished through the law, which was given four hundred thirty years

---

[16] This verse does not say the affliction was 430 years, but rather the "sojourning," (a temporary residing as another's guest) of those who dwelt in Egypt, was 430 years.

[17] This verse does not say that the affliction was 430 years, but rather the law of the covenant was enacted 430 years after it was promised. Observation: Scriptural variance - neither the MLV nor the NCE bibles join the KJV to include "in Christ" in their translations.

afterwards, so that the promise would come to nothing.

In St. Joseph New Catholic Edition [NCE] (for possible clarification):

> Now I mean this: The Law which was made four hundred thirty years later does not annul the covenant which was ratified by God, so as to make the promise void. (NCE Bible footnote: [p245] "3-ver.17. At this time the Law was given to Moses.")

It should be noted here that Archbishop Ussher reasoned "After he [Joseph] died, the Hebrews were held in bondage by the Egyptians 144 years[18]. Therefore, the whole time which the Hebrews spent in Egypt was 215 years, starting from the time that Jacob and his sons went down into Egypt." It appears that Archbishop Ussher halved the scripturally claimed 430-year period.[19]

My calculations equal -1440BC for the approximate start time of the Affliction to the start of the Temple construction at -960BC.

-1440BC less -960BC = 480 years.

It seems apparent that the scriptures naming the 400/430 prophecies cannot be rationally calculated. Either there is more to them than what is biblically included in the timeline, or they are simply in error. I calculate the period from the time of Joseph's death to the Exodus at 172 years, Ussher calculated 144 years for the same period.

---

[18] My calculations for this book have it estimated at 172 years.

[19] See p.137 for Ussher's stance.

4d. The Exodus

Birth of Moses

There is no unanimity on the birth of Moses. Some have placed the date to somewhere in the 14th or 13th century **BCE (1399-1200 BCE)**. Others:

- Ancient.eu/Moses cites "c. **1400 BCE.**" *[viewed 29Feb20]*
- En.Wikipedia.org/wiki/Moses *[viewed 02Jun2015]* states
  - "Rabbinical Judaism calculated a lifespan of Moses corresponding to **1391–1271 BCE;**
  - Jerome gives **1592** BCE, and
  - James Ussher **1571 BCE** as his birth year."
- https://www.britannica.com/contributor/Dewey-M-Beegle/220 *[viewed 29Feb20]* provides an impressive article, wherein he reports possible archeological evidences of the "destruction of the cities" at about 1250BCE, concluding the Exodus began about 1290BCE. Since Moses was 80 years old then, it would set his birth in the year **1370BC.**

When did the Exodus begin?

Researching online articles, one finds all sorts of ideas, each backing their conclusions with impressive thinking and evaluations.

Perhaps some of these theories were motivated by the results one gets when trying to squeeze in the birth years of the 400 years (or 430 years) + the 480 years (= 910 years) between the start of Abraham's prophecy regarding the onset of the affliction and Solomon's temple construction inauguration. This period consists of 13 patriarchal fathers (Isaac, Jacob, Judas, Phares, Esrom, Aram, Aminadab, Naasson, Salman, Booz, Obed, Jesse, and David), and parts of two others (Abraham and Solomon). The average for all of them would be either 60 (with all 15) or 70 (with 13) birth year averages, in spite of the preceding Arphaxad-Nahor average of 31.4 years. If one discounts Abraham, Isaac, and Jacob (who already had his children by the time he sojourns to Egypt and begin there with the affliction, we have only 11 fathers all with a birth year average of 75.8 years. Why would the birth-year average jump to nearly 76 years from a previous 31.4-year average, particularly when David lived to be only 70 and Solomon but 59-80?

As a result, some have deduced the actual time in Egypt was not 400 or 430 but rather only 215 years. It may further be observed in these evaluations that other theorists are also motivated by an urgrund insisting the Bible is perfect.

Aaron and Naashon.

Aaron, the brother of Moses, married Elisheba, the sister of Naasson *(aka Naashon, Nahshon)*.

> And Aaron took him Elisheba, daughter of Amminadab, sister of Naashon, to wife; *(Exo. 6:23)*

Naasson is in the direct genealogical line of descent between Jesus and Adam. Therefore, having an idea about when Naasson was born, we might also conjecture that Moses was likewise born around the same time. Therefore, it is reasonable to consider all of them as contemporaries, of nearly the same age, perhaps plus/minus ten years. (Thus, Moses is a kind of a great, great, grand uncle to Jesus.)

Aaron was about three years older than Moses.

> And Moses *was* fourscore years old, and Aaron fourscore and three years old, when they spake unto Pharaoh. *(Exo. 7:7)*

Aaron and Naashon might also have had children, hidden from the Pharaoh. Likely, having not left Egypt like Moses was forced to do, they might have attempted to have their children while yet young. But due to the Affliction and their genealogical heritage, they rather may have waited until they were older before quietly starting their family, to not arouse suspicion, as the Pharaoh was still intent on suppressing Israeli reproduction. Naashon's patriarchal son Salman, destined to be of the lineage of the Saviour as Naashon was, could have been a teenager, or older, by then.

Moses.

Time passes, the Israelites multiply, until we come to Moses. Now, the scriptures imply that the Pharaoh of that time was being more successful in "casting out" the "young children" (probably killing many). Raised in the palaces of the Pharaoh to maturity, according to Josephus, Moses found himself in the role of defending Egypt against invading Ethiopians. Ultimately Moses' Egyptian army finds itself at the gates of the Ethiopian royal city of Saba (aka Mero). It is at this time Moses meets, bargains with, and marries an Ethiopian woman, **Tharbis**, daughter of the Ethiopian king, after she delivers up the city to him (see note 23). It is not known if Moses and Tharbis had any offspring.

AND Miriam and Aaron spake against Moses because of the Ethiopian woman whom he had married: for **he had married an Ethiopian[20] woman**. *(Num. 12:1; ba)*

Moses next visits his kin when he is 40 years old (see v23). Likely, at this time he would have met his brother Aaron and Aaron's wife Elisheba, and her brother Naashon, all married perhaps years earlier.

The disciple Stephen explained events of this time, quoted here in part.

> 6 And God spake on this wise, That his [Abraham's] seed should sojourn in a strange land; and that they should bring them into bondage, and **entreat *them* evil four hundred years. ...**
>
> 17 But when the time of the promise drew nigh, which God had sworn to Abraham, the people grew and multiplied in Egypt,
>
> 18 Till another king arose, which knew not Joseph.
>
> 19 The same dealt subtilly with our kindred, and evil entreated **our fathers, so that they cast out their young children, to the end they might not live.**
>
> 20 In which time Moses was born, and was exceeding fair, and nourished up in his father's house three months:
>
> 21 And when he was cast out, Pharaoh's daughter took him up, and nourished him for her own son.
>
> 22 And Moses was learned in all the wisdom of the Egyptians, and was mighty in words and in deeds.
>
> 23 And **when he was full forty years old,** it came into his heart to visit his brethren the children of Israel.

---

[20] Regarding the word *Ethiopia*, "This is the word used by the Greeks and Romans for the Hebrew name *Cush*. Cush was the son of Ham, and his descendants occupied the country to the S. of Egypt, ..." YAC, p308. But see note 23. *Ddd Note: Tharbis is not mentioned by name in the Scriptures.*

24 And seeing one *of them* suffer wrong, he defended *him,* and avenged him that was oppressed, and smote the Egyptian:

25 For he supposed his brethren would have understood how that God by his hand would deliver them: but they understood not.

26 And the next day he shewed himself unto them as they strove, and would have set them at one again, saying, Sirs, ye are brethren; why do ye wrong one to another?

27 But he that did his neighbour wrong thrust him away, saying, Who made thee a ruler and a judge over us?

28 Wilt thou kill me, as thou diddest the Egyptian yesterday?

29 Then fled Moses at this saying, and was a stranger in the land of Madian, where he begat two sons.

30 And **when forty years**[21] **were expired**, there appeared to him in the wilderness of mount Sina an angel of the Lord in a flame of fire in a bush. *(Acts 7:6, 17-30)*

Fleeing for his life (v29), Moses likely leaves behind his Ethiopian wife Tharbis (and any children he might have had with her) and ends up in the land of Midian. There he meets and marries Zipporah, the daughter of a Kenite, named Jethro, the priest of Midian, and has two sons by her.

21 And Moses was content to dwell with the man: and he gave Moses **Zipporah** his daughter.

---

[21] *DDD Note: notice how many times the magical number "40" comes up in the Scriptures? Consider an explanation given later in this book. regarding rounded numbers, p.63.*

22 And she bare *him* a son, and he called his name **Gershom**: for he said, I have been a stranger in a strange land. *(Exo. 2:21,22; ba)*

3 And her two sons; of which the name of the one *was* **Gershom**; for he said, I have been an alien in a strange land:
4 And the name of the other *was* **Eliezer**; for the God of my father, *said he, was* mine help, and delivered me from the sword of Pharaoh: *(Exo. 18: 3,4; ba)*

And the children of **the Kenite, Moses' father in law***, went up out of the city of palm trees with the children of Judah into the wilderness of Judah, which *lieth* in the south of Arad; and they went and dwelt among the people. *(Judges 1:16; ba; *Jethro)*

Forty more years lapse, and 80 year old Moses (along with his second wife and their two boys) returns to Egypt as a prophet, seer, and revelator to the children of Israel to seek their exodus from the Pharaoh and go to the land of Israel's inheritance.
The Kenites were among the original inhabitants of the land that Abraham was told would become the land of Israel. They were not regarded as Ethiopians.

18 In the same day the LORD made a covenant with Abram, saying, Unto thy seed have I given this land, from the river of Egypt unto the great river, the river Euphrates:
19 **The Kenites**, and the Kenizzites, and the Kadmonites, *(Gen. 15:18, 19; ba)*

The Bible Dictionary of the Four Standard Works offers the following glimpse of the Kenites.

Kenites. Probably a Midianite tribe, descended from Abraham by his wife Keturah. Moses' marriage with the daughter of Jethro, a prince and priest of Midian, was also a cause of the long-standing friendship between the Kenites and Israelites (Num. 24:21–22; Judg. 1:16; 4:11, 17; 5:24; 1 Sam. 15:6; 27:10; 30:29).

> 1 THEN again Abraham took a wife, and her name *was* **Keturah**.
> 2 And she bare him Zimran, and Jokshan, and Medan, and **Midian**, and Ishbak, and Shuah. *(Gen.25:1,2; ba)*

However, that creates another question. How can the Kenites descend from Abraham's wife Keturah, who he married late in his life, when they already existed at the time the Lord made the Covenant with him *(see p39)*? Since the Kenites co-existed with Abraham, it is more likely they descended from someone earlier than Abraham, from one of Noah's first two sons, Shem or Japheth. But the forefathers of Jethro at some point integrated into the Kenite tribe of the Midians. There is much speculation about the origin of the Kenites, even theorizing their name came from Cain. Others believe it came from Kenan, son of Enoch.[22]

> Noah made another promise at this time, and he said, "God shall enlarge Japheth, and He shall dwell in the house or tent of Shem."[19] What is the house or tent of Shem? The House of Israel. Therefore, descendants of Japheth shall be enlarged, and they shall be permitted to dwell in the House of Israel. Therefore, we call the descendants of Japheth the children of the adoption. Now, who are the descendants of

---

[22] See 1 Chron. 1:2.

Japheth? The descendants of Japheth are in all of Europe. They are in America. They are in Japan and Korea, They are in India, and all of these people can be traced. Footnote [19] quotes Gen. 9:27: *"God shall enlarge Japheth, and he shall dwell in the tents of Shem; and Canaan shall be his servant."* *(FWP, 16)*

Nevertheless, we may reasonably conclude Zipporah was not the Ethiopian woman that Miriam and Aaron complained to Moses about, quoted earlier. Therefore, the Ethiopian woman was the first of *two* wives of Moses. The ancient historian Josephus narrates Moses marrying an Ethiopian woman named Tharbis.[23] who was the daughter of the Ethiopian king.

It is reputed that the people of Cush (Ethiopia, see note 20) are descended from Noah's third son Ham.

And the sons of Ham; Cush, and Mizraim, and Phut, and Canaan. *(Gen. 10:6)*

---

[23] See https://en.wikipedia.org/wiki/Tharbis *[viewed May2018] referring to "Antiquities of the Jews, p.61." by Flavius Josephus. Excerpted from Project Gutenberg's The Antiquities of the Jews, by Flavius Josephus as follows.* "However, while Moses was uneasy at the army's lying idle, [for the enemies durst not come to a battle,] this accident happened:—**Tharbis was the daughter of the king of the Ethiopians**: she happened to see Moses as he led the army near the walls, and fought with great courage; and admiring the subtilty of his undertakings, and believing him to be the author of the Egyptians' success, when they had before despaired of recovering their liberty, and to be the occasion of the great danger the Ethiopians were in, when they had before boasted of their great achievements, she fell deeply in love with him; and upon the prevalancy of that passion, sent to him the most faithful of all her servants to discourse with him about their marriage. He thereupon accepted the offer, on condition she would procure the delivering up of the city; and gave her the assurance of an oath to take her to his wife; and that when he had once taken possession of the city, he would not break his oath to her. No sooner was the agreement made, but it took effect immediately; and when Moses had cut off the Ethiopians, he gave thanks to God, and consummated his marriage, and led the Egyptians back to their own land." *(Book II, Chapter 10)* Also, another excerpt from *Antiquities of the Jews* by Josephus: "The reader is to remember that Cush is not Ethiopia, but Arabia. See Bochart, B. IV. ch. 2." *(Book VIII, Chapter 15, Footnotes 30).* But see previous note 20 for another point of view.

According to the Book of Abraham, Ham's wife was Egyptus. Their daughter, also named Egyptus, discovered the land known as Egypt.

21 Now this king of Egypt was a descendant from the loins of Ham, and was a partaker of the blood of the Canaanites by birth.

22 From this descent sprang all the Egyptians, and thus the blood of the Canaanites was preserved in the land.

23 **The land of Egypt being first discovered by a woman, who was the daughter of Ham, and the daughter of Egyptus**, which in the Chaldean signifies Egypt, which signifies that which is forbidden;

24 When this woman discovered the land it was under water, who afterward settled her sons in it; and thus, from Ham, sprang that race which preserved the curse in the land.

25 Now the first government of Egypt was established by Pharaoh, the eldest son of Egyptus, the daughter of Ham, and it was after the manner of the government of Ham, which was patriarchal.

26 Pharaoh, being a righteous man, established his kingdom and judged his people wisely and justly all his days, seeking earnestly to imitate that order established by the fathers in the first generations, in the days of the first patriarchal reign, even in the reign of Adam, and also of Noah, his father, who blessed him with the blessings of the earth, and with the blessings of wisdom, but cursed him as pertaining to the Priesthood.

27 Now, **Pharaoh being of that lineage by which he could not have the right of Priesthood**, notwithstanding the Pharaohs would fain claim it from Noah, through Ham, therefore my father was led away by their idolatry; *(Abr. 1:21-27; ba)*

Since Jethro, Moses' father-in-law, was a recognized priest of the Midians, living in the land taken over by Israel, and as a priest therefore having the priesthood (see Exo.18:12), he would not have been from the descendants of Ham, who were not permitted to have the priesthood *at that time*, including those in Ethiopia.

> 6 And Joseph died, and all his brethren, and all that generation.
> 7 And the children of Israel were fruitful, and increased abundantly, and multiplied, and waxed exceeding mighty; and the land was filled with them.
> 8 Now there arose up a new king over Egypt, which knew not Joseph.
> 9 And he said unto his people, Behold, the people of the children of Israel *are* more and mightier than we:
> 10 Come on, let us deal wisely with them; lest they multiply, and it come to pass, that, when there falleth out any war, they join also unto our enemies, and fight against us, and *so* get them up out of the land.
> 11 Therefore they did set over them taskmasters to afflict them with their burdens. And they built for Pharaoh treasure cities, Pithom and Raamses.
> 12 **But the more they afflicted them, the more they multiplied and grew**. And they were grieved because of the children of Israel. *(Exo. 1:6-12; ba)*

We see that oppressing the Israelites did not deter them from having children, and lots of them, despite "casting out" many.

We know how Moses was "cast out," set adrift by his mother to save his life, as the king wanted male children to be killed upon birth. But the king was not successful in the case of Moses.

15 And the king of Egypt spake to the Hebrew midwives, of which the name of the one *was* Shiphrah, and the name of the other Puah:

16 And he said, When ye do the office of a midwife to the Hebrew women, and see *them* upon the stools; if it *be* a son, then ye shall kill him: but if it *be* a daughter, then she shall live.

17 But the midwives feared God, and did not as the king of Egypt commanded them, but saved the men children alive.

18 And the king of Egypt called for the midwives, and said unto them, Why have ye done this thing, and have saved the men children alive?

19 And the midwives said unto Pharaoh, Because the Hebrew women *are* not as the Egyptian women; for they *are* lively, and are delivered ere the midwives come in unto them.

20 Therefore God dealt well with the midwives: and the people multiplied, and waxed very mighty. *(Exo.1:15-20)*

Leaving Egypt.

Moses, Aaron and Naasson were now at the crossroads of leaving Egypt with their wives and children. As they all were at that time about 80+/- years of age, their children would now have also been adults, married and having their children as well.

Naasson, also about 80 years of age at the time of the Exodus, may have had his son Salman some 20-50+ years earlier.

480 years.

The Scriptures calculate 480 years between the start of the Exodus and the start of Solomon's Temple being built. Is this feasible?

> AND it came to pass **in the four hundred and eightieth year** after the children of Israel were come out of the land of Egypt, in the fourth year of Solomon's reign over Israel, in the month Zif, which *is* the second month, that he began to build the house of the LORD. *(1 Kings 6:1; ba)*

480 years – 51 years of age to David's wife Bathsheba having Solomon – 24 years from Solomon's birth to the start of building the temple (51+24=75 years) = (480-75) **405 birth years to split between the remaining 4 fathers**. Naasson was quite active after the return to the land of Israel. Likely, Naasson already had begotten his oldest son Salman back in Egypt.

Thus the 405 years must be spread between **Salman***, **Boaz***, **Obed,** and **Jesse.** That equals 101+ years apiece for each having the first-born oldest son. And by the time of the Exodus, Salman was probably going to have Boaz soon. So, we cannot give him another 101+ years to do that. Just not realistic.   **aka Salmon, Booz*

Remember how Abraham reacted when he learned at age 99 he was finally going to have a son? And this was at a time when it was common to live well beyond 100 years of age. Though these ancients lived well past 100 years of age, yet by the time they approached that centennial age, they regarded themselves past the childbearing age.

Then Abraham fell upon his face, and laughed, and said in his heart, **Shall *a child* be born unto him that is an hundred years old?** and shall Sarah, that is ninety years old, bear? *(Gen. 17:17)*

And now, we are to accept the idea that Salman, Booz, Obed, and Jesse *all* had their firstborn about an age at or greater than Abraham did? We must not forget that by the time of David and Solomon, men were dying of natural causes about the age of 59-70. Something is askew.

5 So Moses the servant of the LORD died there in the land of Moab, according to the word of the LORD.

6 And he buried him in a valley in the land of Moab, over against Beth-peor: but no man knoweth of his sepulchre unto this day.

7 And **Moses *was* an hundred and twenty years old when he died**: his eye was not dim, nor his natural force abated. *(Deut. 34:5-7; ba)*

Birth of King David

Moving along down the chronology, we come to King David. When was King David born? Nobody knows for sure.

- Ussher says **1085 BC**.
- Some online report the Jewish calendar calculating the date to be 2854 (**907BC**).
- Others, such as the Encyclopedia Britannica *(Britannica.combiography/David, viewed 29Feb20)* cites **1000BC**.
- *(Bibleque.net/answer/887, viewed 29Feb20)* says **1041BC**.
- *(Ancient.eu/King_David, viewed 29Feb20)* provides two dates: **1035BCE** and "around **1000BCE**."

Now David *was* the son of that Ephrathite of Beth-lehem-judah, whose name *was* **Jesse; and he had eight sons: and the man went among men *for* an**

> **old man** in the days of Saul. ... 14 And David *was* the youngest: ... *(1 Sam. 17:12,14; ba)*

While at least eight years may have intervened in order for Jesse to have his eight sons, it would only mean Jesse was eight years older when David was born than when he had his first son, and then later became regarded as an old man in the days of Saul. Still, he was likely older than the average till then.

Conventional chronologies generally regard Solomon to be about 20-24 years of age when he began building the temple.

Trying to find a balance during the period between Moses and Solomon is difficult. The scriptures figure 480 years between the Exodus and when the House of the Lord began to be built. But there are too few patriarchs available in that block to reasonably distribute so many years.

Testing out numerous propositions from information available in scriptural and other sources, I finally settled on 3740BC for the creation as previously stated (p.30), with the affliction beginning after Judah and Joseph died; the four generations of Judah, Phares, Esrom and Aram *before* the affliction probably enjoyed an earlier birth age closer to Period 2 of the Arphaxad-Nahor Seven. Here, I averaged their birth age at <38 years, the same as the 26 patriarchs from Roboam (Rehoboam) through Joseph.

During the Affliction the birth ages likely spiked. I averaged that oppressed group having still longer longevities, from Aminadab to Obed, at 59+ years.

These two averages bring David's birth in at 1035BC. This results in a reasonable <38-year average for the remaining 26 patriarchs down to the Christ, the average for them being the same as for the Judah-Aram four. These four lived when the longevity was declining, but still in the low hundreds, like Moses who lived to be 120.

David lived to be only about 70 years of age:

> David *was* thirty years old when he began to reign, *and* he reigned forty years. *(2 Sam. 5:4)*

Ussher states David was 51 years old when he begat Solomon, which is reasonable. (Solomon was the tenth known son born to David.) Conventional chronologies state Solomon lived anywhere from 59 to 80 years of age, before he died of natural causes. Like his father David, Solomon reigned about 40 years.

Scripture only says:

> 42 And the time that Solomon reigned in Jerusalem over all Israel *was* forty years.
>
> 43 And **Solomon slept with his fathers**, and was buried in the city of David his father: and Rehoboam his son reigned in his stead. *(1 Kings 11:42, 43; ba)*

The Death of David

> 1 NOW king David was **old *and* stricken in years**; and they covered him with clothes, but **he gat no heat**.
>
> 2 Wherefore his servants said unto him, Let there be sought for my lord the king a young virgin: and let her stand before the king, and let her cherish him, and let her lie in thy bosom, that my lord the king may get heat.
>
> 3 So they sought for a fair damsel throughout all the coasts of Israel, and found Abishag a Shunammite, and brought her to the king.

4 And the damsel *was* very fair, and cherished the king, and ministered to him: but the king knew her not. ...
39 And Zadok the priest took an horn of oil out of the tabernacle, and anointed Solomon. And they blew the trumpet; and all the people said, God save king Solomon. *(1 Kings 1:4; ba)*

1 NOW the days of David drew nigh that he should die; and he charged Solomon his son, saying,
2 **I go the way of all the earth**: be thou strong therefore, and shew thyself a man;
3 And keep the charge of the LORD thy God, to walk in his ways, to keep his statutes, and his commandments, and his judgments, and his testimonies, as it is written in the law of Moses, that thou mayest prosper in all that thou doest, and whithersoever thou turnest thyself:
4 That the LORD may continue his word which he spake concerning me, saying, If thy children take heed to their way, to walk before me in truth with all their heart and with all their soul, there shall not fail thee (said he) a man on the throne of Israel. ...
10 **So David slept with his fathers**, and was buried in the city of David. *(1 Kings 2:1-4; ba)*

As the above scripture attests, King David was nearing death when he made Solomon his successor. Dates and times for the births and deaths of Moses, David and Solomon are all subject to much hypothesis and speculation. Even the oft quoted number "40" is highly suspect, which leads us to the next subject "Scriptural Mathematical Errors."

4e. Scriptural Mathematical Errors

There are a number of mathematical errors in both the KJV and the JST of the Bible. One error pertains to when Arphaxad was born and how old his father Shem was when he was begotten. Archbishop Ussher took a few liberties to tweak these biblical errors into non-errors. Another error is in the JST. How Shem became elder to Japheth when it records Japheth being elder to Shem is not explained *(see p.61)*.

Let us start with certain facts as laid out in the King James Version.

> Gen. 5:32 [KJV] And Noah was **five hundred years old: and Noah begat Shem**, Ham, and Japheth.

> Gen. 7:6 KJV] And **Noah** *was* **six hundred years old when the flood** of waters was upon the earth.

> Gen. 11:10 [KJV] These *are* the generations of Shem: **Shem** *was* **an hundred years old, and begat Arphaxad two years after the flood.**

Noah was 500 years old when he begat (brought a child into existence) Shem. And Noah was 600 when the Flood came. 600-500 = 100. That makes Shem 100 years old when the Flood came.

Shem was 100 years old when he begat Arphaxad, which happened two years *after* the Flood. Therefore, Shem was 98 years old when the Flood came, and not 100 as the Bible also says above.

To get an agreement in the scriptures regarding this period, we might consider tweaking the facts that some of the verses convey.

If we change some of the data provided by the *KJV* Bible,

Gen. 5:32 [KJV] And Noah was ~~five hundred~~ [502] years old: and Noah begat Shem, Ham, and Japheth. *(Ddd note: this one was favored by Ussher)*

Gen. 7:6 KJV] And **Noah *was* six hundred years old when the flood** of waters was upon the earth.

Gen. 11:10 [KJV] These *are* the generations of Shem: **Shem *was* an hundred years old, and begat Arphaxad two years after the flood.**

or

Gen. 5:32 [KJV] And Noah was **five hundred years old: and Noah begat Shem, Ham, and Japheth.**

Gen. 7:6 KJV] And **Noah *was* ~~six hundred~~ [598] years old when the flood** of waters was upon the earth.

Gen. 11:10 [KJV] These *are* the generations of Shem: **Shem *was* an hundred years old, and begat Arphaxad two years after the flood.**

or

Gen. 5:32 [KJV] And Noah was **five hundred years old: and Noah begat Shem, Ham, and Japheth.**

Gen. 7:6 KJV] And **Noah *was* six hundred years old when the flood** of waters was upon the earth.

Gen. 11:10 [KJV] These *are* the generations of Shem: **Shem *was* ~~an hundred~~ [102] years old, and begat Arphaxad two years after the flood.**

then we have a mathematically correct account.

While solving some obvious errors, such as Noah having triplets, but still adding to the confusion, Joseph Smith's translation offers these facts.

Gen. 7:85 [JST] And Noah was four hundred and fifty years old, and begat Japheth, and forty-two years afterwards, he begat Shem **[Noah was 450+42=492 years old when he begat Shem]**,

Gen. 8:33 [JST] And Noah was six hundred **[600]** years old when the flood of waters was upon the earth. **[600-492=108. Shem then was 108 years old when the flood was upon the earth].**

Gen. 11:7 [JST] And Shem being an hundred **[100 years]** years old, begat Arphaxad two years after the flood **[100-2=98. Shem was 98 years old when the flood was upon the earth]**;

If we change some of the data provided by the *JST* Bible,

Gen. 7:85 [JST] And Noah was four hundred and fifty years old, and begat Japheth, and forty-two years afterwards, he begat Shem **[Noah was 450+42=492years old when he begat Shem]**,

Gen. 8:33 [JST] And **Noah was** ~~six hundred~~ **[590] years old when the flood** of waters was upon the earth **[590-492=98 years after the birth of Shem]**. (*Ddd Note: this one favored by Doddridge. 590 instead of 600 = 2094BC instead of 2084BC)*

Gen. 11:7 [JST] And **Shem** being **an hundred years old, begat Arphaxad two years after the flood; [98+2=100 years]**

or

Gen. 7:85 [JST] And Noah was four hundred and fifty years old, and begat Japheth, and forty-two years afterwards, he begat Shem **[Noah was 450+42=492years old when he begat Shem]**,

Gen. 8:33 [JST] And Noah was six hundred **[600]** years old when the flood of waters was upon the earth. **[600-492=108. Shem then was 108 years old when the flood was upon the earth].**

Gen. 11:7 [JST] And **Shem** being ~~an hundred~~ **[110 years] years old, begat Arphaxad two years after the flood; [600-492=108+2=110}.**

then we have a mathematically correct account.

The JST figure of 492 years in Gen.7:85 [JST] is quite specific, thus it appears that was a definite inspirational move. It appears that other verses were not improved upon. Further it solves the problem of Noah having all three sons in the self-same year.

> Gen. 5:32 [KJV] And Noah was **five hundred years old: and Noah begat Shem, Ham, and Japheth.**

> Gen. 7:85 [JST] And Noah was **four hundred and fifty years old, and begat Japheth, and forty-two years afterwards, he begat Shem, and when he was five hundred years old, he begat Ham.**

Shem's Birthright.

> Gen. 7:85 [JST] And Noah was **four hundred and fifty years old,** and **begat Japheth, and forty-two years afterwards,** he **begat Shem,**

> Gen. 10:12 [JST] Unto **Shem also, which was the elder,** children were born; ...

The first verse shows Japheth as the elder to Shem by 42 years. The last JST verse states *Shem was the elder,* which is consistent with Christ's genealogy that shows him to have the birthright in the Patriarchal line-up and not Japheth.

> Gen. 10:2 [JST] The **sons of Japheth**; Gomer, and Magog, Madai, and Javan, and Tubal, and Meschech, and Tiras.

This verse shows that Japheth, at least for a number of years, lived to have offspring.

> Gen. 9:27 KJV; 9:31 [JST] God shall enlarge **Japheth, and he shall dwell in the tents of Shem**; and Canaan shall be his servant.

This verse reinforces the idea that *the elder Japheth* by age lived after the Flood long enough to enlarge his family, but nevertheless Japheth was *junior* to Shem in birthright, he to dwell under Shem's roof. Scriptures show he was righteous but do not explain how he lost his birthright to Shem.

Mistakes in the JST? Here is what Robert J Matthews correctly concludes.

> It is evident from the manuscripts prepared by the Prophet and his scribes, and also from the statements by the Prophet himself, that he did not correct all of the passages that could be corrected in the Bible. **Hence, the new translation is not finished. It is not a perfect Bible.** *(By Robert J. Matthews, Assistant Professor of Ancient Scripture, Brigham Young University, Dec 1972; ba;*
> *https://www.lds.org/ensign/1972/12/joseph-smiths-inspired-translation-of-the-bible?lang=eng)*

Joseph Smith's spreading out the births of the sons Shem, Japheth, and Ham makes more sense than the KJV showing Noah having triplets in his 500th year or that he was polygamous. Whatever figures I use to correct the scriptural exposés will be at odds with other equally plausible possibilities. We are not reviewing a lot of years here. So, I will just leave it as it is for now, namely the various Ussher Bible sources for the Ussher Chronology and Joseph Smith Translation for the Doddridge Chronology.

4f. Scriptural rounded numbers.

These *biblically* adduced even numbers 40, 100, 400, 500, 600, etc. in many cases may be just rounded estimates and not exacts.

There are 157 quotes in the Bible using "forty," but only a few with "forty and" (one through nine) quantities, more in conjunction with another number; and only one 39 as a total. It is evident and can be defended that the number *forty* is meant in many cases as being a proxy number for an unknown actual by the original scribe. Likewise, the numbers 480, which is 40 x 12 and 400 (40 x 10) might well also fall into that category. Moses living to the age of 120 is 40 x 3, and so on. 40 might represent anything from 21 to 60, including 40.

6,000-year mortal existence

-

3,740 BC

=

2,260 years to the end of the mortal existence

-

A period of time (70 years) for the "days shortened"
(Matt. 24:22)

=

The time of the Second coming (2,190 AD).

It is now at this writing, the year 2020. Doddridge guesstimates the *days shortened* at 70 years (1% of 7,000 years of the temporal existence) in length. The Doddridge Chronology therefore figures another 170 years before the Second Coming. But then, maybe the days shortened are really up to 240 years (6000-3740-240 = 2020)!

4g. Chronological Comparisons

The scriptures show us that the first 2,098 years (see p.22) of the 7,000-year temporal existence lapsed from Adam until Isaac begat Jacob. Thereafter data becomes sketchy.

Isaac was 60 years old, when Jacob was born,

> And after that came his brother out, and his hand took hold on Esau's heel; and his name was called **Jacob**: and **Isaac *was* threescore years old** when she bare them. *(Gen. 25:26)*

Scriptures say Jacob [with Leah] begat Judas (Judah), who was the fourth of the twelve sons of Jacob,

> Abraham begat Isaac; and Isaac begat Jacob; and **Jacob begat Judas** and his brethren; *(Matt. 1:2)*

but they do not tell us when that happened.

Consequently, we do not know *exactly* how many more years of our pre-Millennial 6,000-year mortal existence lapsed between Jacob and the birth of his son Judas. And likewise, through most of the other patriarchs down to the time of Jesus' birth.

6,000 years minus 2,098 years = 3,902 years until the Millennium begins. Now, how many of the 3,902 years have lapsed until this present time? We learn the following from the Doctrine and Covenants.

*Revelation on Church Organization and Government, given through Joseph Smith the Prophet, **April 1830**. HC 1:64–70. Preceding his record of this revelation the Prophet wrote: "We obtained of him [Jesus Christ] the following, by the spirit of prophecy and revelation; which not only gave us much information, but also pointed out to us the precise day upon which, according* *to his will and commandment, we should proceed to organize his Church once more here upon the earth."* ... THE rise of the Church of Christ in these last days, **being one thousand eight hundred and thirty years since the coming of our Lord and Savior Jesus Christ in the flesh**, it being regularly organized and established agreeable to the laws of our country, by the will and commandments of God, in the fourth month, and on the sixth day of the month which is called April— *(D&C 20:1; ba; see also pp.91,92)*

This scripture disputes the idea of Christ's actual birth being in 5BC, as cited in Ussher's Chronology (see p.140).

3,902 minus 1,830 years = 2,072 years still unaccounted for. Most of the 2,072 years are from Judas to Jesus' birth and the rest are from the present time until the Millennium. Those are the years we need to still account for.

The chart on page 67 compares the two chronologies, Doddridge and Ussher, and includes the period from Judas to Jesus. The chart begins with the period after the longer living patriarchs, starting with Arphaxad and then down through Joseph. Noteworthy is the Ussher Chronology pressing in King David's birth at 1085BC. To do this, a bottleneck increase of the birth average requires squeezing in a high, rather untenable 66-year average between Judas and Obed, more than double the preceding Arphaxad-Nahor average of 31.4 years. But doing so allows the extra centuries to be added to the dating so the 4004BC advent for Adam can be touted, rather than something closer to a more tenable 3740BC start for Adam.

On the other hand, the Doddridge Chronology also does not get down to the 31.4 years, but does get closer, with its 37.85-year average, due to Biblical troublesome histories.

After King David, Ussher's 40-year average, from Solomon to Joseph averages slightly higher than the Arphaxad-Nahor average, yet is reasonable as the Israelites during much of that period lived in turmoil.

Note. Averaging is performed by determining the sum of a set of numbers and dividing the result by the quantity of numbers added. Example: 4+3+4+5+9+5 = 30 / 6 numbers = an average of 5.

Doddridge's 37.85 year average (Doddridge Chronology Table, p.68) also comes in yet a bit closer to the Arphaxad-Nahor average, but still a little higher for the same reason of turmoil being experienced.

Continual wars, scatterings, famines, etc. would likely drive up the birth-age average. The following scripture certainly suggests a higher birth-age for some.

> 11 And Josias begat Jechonias and his brethren, **about the time they were carried away to Babylon**:
> 12 And **after they were brought to Babylon**, Jechonias begat Salathiel; and Salathiel begat Zorobabel; *(Matt. 1:11,12; ba)*

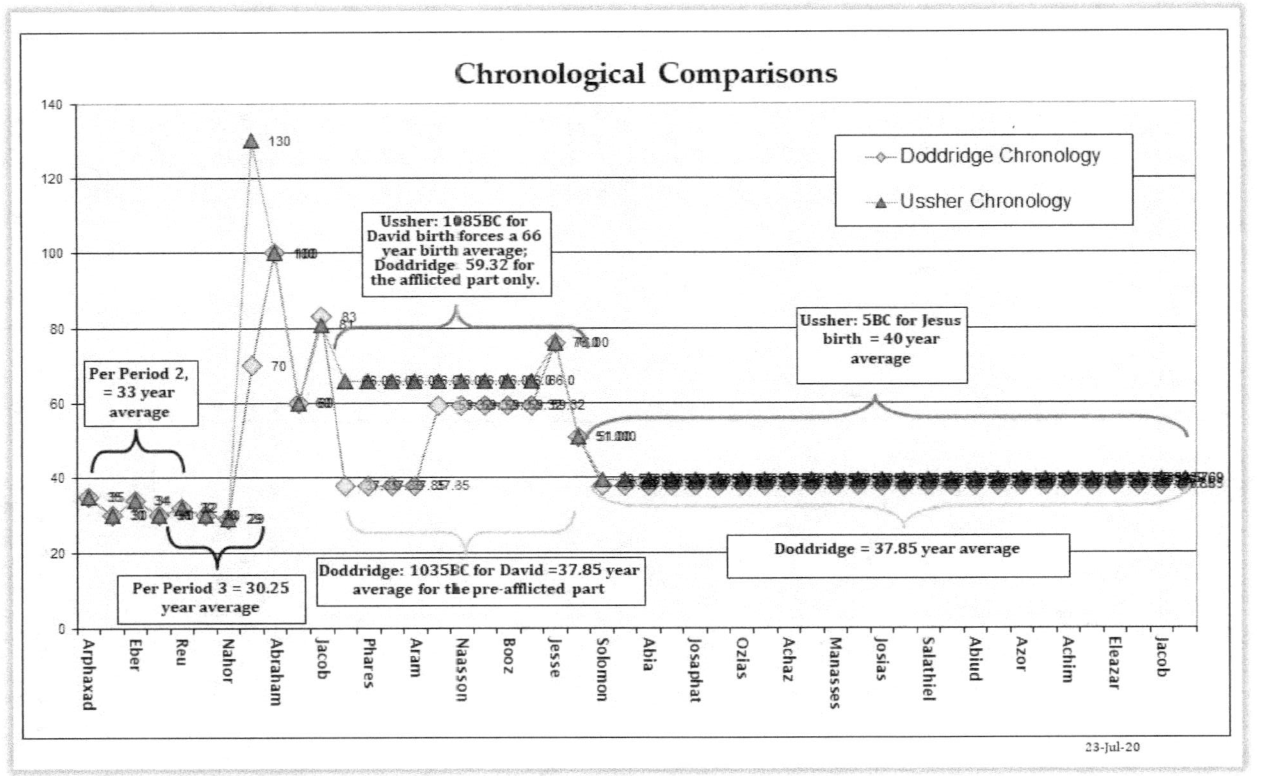

Chronological Comparisons
Doddridge Chronology
Ussher Chronology
140
120
100
80
60
40
20
0
130
70
Ussher: 1085BC for David birth forces a 66 year birth average; Doddridge 59.32 for the afflicted part only.
Ussher: 5BC for Jesus birth = 40 year average
Per Period 2, = 33 year average
Per Period 3 = 30.25 year average
Doddridge: 1035BC for David =37.85 year average for the pre-afflicted part
Doddridge = 37.85 year average
Arphaxad
Eber
Reu
Nahor
Abraham
Jacob
Phares
Aram
Naasson
Booz
Jesse
Solomon
Abia
Josaphat
Ozias
Achaz
Manasses
Josias
Salathiel
Abiud
Azor
Achim
Eleazar
Jacob
23-Jul-20

Doddridge Chronology 2nd Edition

No.		Age at Son's Birth	Year Born	Patriarch		No.		Age at Son's Birth	Year Born	Patriarch	
		Period 1 (Avg 115.60)							*-1268*	*Exodus*	
1	60	130	-3740	**Adam**		30	31	*59*	-1230	Booz	
2	59	105	-3610	Seth					*-1228*	*Moses dies: age 120*	
3	58	90	-3505	Enos		31	30	*59*	-1170	Obed	
4	57	70	-3415	Cainan				*Period 7 (Avg 63.50)*			
5	56	65	-3345	Mahalaleel		32	29	*76*	-1111	Jesse	308
6	55	162	-3280	Jared		33	28	*51*	**-1035**	**David**	
7	54	65	-3118	Enoch				*Period 8 (Avg 37.85)*			
8	53	187	-3053	Methusaleh		34	27	*38*	-984	Solomon	
9	52	182	-2866	Lamech					*-965*	*David dies: age 70*	
10	51	**492**	-2684	**Noah**					*-960*	*Temple Construct*	
11	50	100	-2192	Shem		35	26	*38*	-946	Roboam	
		Period 2 (Avg 33.00)				36	25	*38*	-908	Abia	
12	49	35	-2092	Arphaxad		37	24	*38*	-870	Asa	
13	48	30	-2057	Salah		38	23	*38*	-833	Josaphat	
14	47	34	-2027	Eber		39	22	*38*	-795	Joram	
		Period 3 (Avg 30.25)				40	21	*38*	-757	Ozias	
15	46	30	-1993	Peleg		41	20	*38*	-719	Joatham	
16	45	32	-1963	Reu		42	19	*38*	-681	Achaz	
17	44	30	-1931	Serug		43	18	*38*	-643	Ezekias	
18	43	29	-1901	Nahor		44	17	*38*	-606	Manasses	
		Period 4 (Avg 78.25)				45	16	*38*	-568	Amon	
19	42	**70**	-1872	Terah		46	15	*38*	-530	Josias	
20	41	**100**	-1802	**Abraham**		47	14	*38*	-492	Jechonias	
21	40	**60**	-1702	**Isaac**		48	13	*38*	-454	Salathiel	
22	39	*83*	-1642	**Jacob**		49	12	*38*	-416	Zorobabel	
		Period 5 (Avg 37.85)				50	11	*38*	-378	Abiud	
23	38	*38*	-1559	Judas		51	10	*38*	-341	Eliakim	
24	37	*38*	-1521	Phares		52	9	*38*	-303	Azor	
25	36	*38*	-1483	Esrom		53	8	*38*	-265	Sadoc	
26	35	*38*	-1445	Aram		54	7	*38*	-227	Achim	
		Period 6 (Avg 59.32)				55	6	*38*	-189	Eliud	
			-1440	*The Affliction*		56	5	*38*	-151	Eleazar	
27	34	*59*	-1408	Aminadab		57	4	*38*	-114	Matthan	
			-1348	*Moses born*		58	3	*38*	-76	Jacob	
28	33	*59*	-1348	Naasson	172	59	2	*38*	-38	Joseph	
29	32	*59*	-1289	Salman		60	1	*38*	0	Jesus	
			Total 480			61	0	2260-70=	**2190**	Second Coming	

It appears that the 480 years cited in 1Kings 6:1 befits the start of the temple construction back to the start of the Affliction rather than the start of the Exodus.

Italics are based on the results of averaging unknown variables. Period 1 average excludes Noah.

6000 mortal existence years - 3740 = 2260 - 70 gestimated shortened years = 2190 for 2nd Coming

Ussher Chronology

No.	Age at Son's Birth	Year Born	Patriarch	No.	Age at Son's Birth	Year Born	Patriarch
	Period 1 (Avg 115.6)				*Period 5&6 (cont.)*		
1 60	130	-4004	**Adam**	30 31	*66*	-1293	Booz
2 59	105	-3874	Seth	31 30	*66*	-1227	Obed
3 58	90	-3769	Enos		*Period 7 (Avg 63.50)*		
4 57	70	-3679	Cainan	32 29	*76*	-1161	Jesse
5 56	65	-3609	Mahalaleel	33 28	*51*	-1085.00	**David**
6 55	162	-3544	Jared		*Period 8 (Avg 39.6)*		
7 54	65	-3382	Enoch	34 27	*40*	-1034	Solomon
8 53	187	-3317	Methusaleh	35 26	*40*	-994	Roboam
9 52	182	-3130	Lamech	36 25	*40*	-955	Abia
10 51	**502**	-2948	**Noah**	37 24	*40*	-915	Asa
11 50	100	-2446	Shem	38 23	*40*	-876	Josaphat
	Period 2 (Avg 33.0)			39 22	*40*	-836	Joram
12 49	35	-2346	Arphaxad	40 21	*40*	-797	Ozias
13 48	30	-2311	Salah	41 20	*40*	-757	Joatham
14 47	34	-2281	Eber	42 19	*40*	-717	Achaz
	Period 3 (Avg 30.25)			43 18	*40*	-678	Ezekias
15 46	30	-2247	Peleg	44 17	*40*	-638	Manasses
16 45	32	-2217	Reu	45 16	*40*	-599	Amon
17 44	30	-2185	Serug	46 15	*40*	-559	Josias
18 43	29	-2155	Nahor	47 14	*40*	-520	Jechonias
	Period 4 (Avg 92.75)			48 13	*40*	-480	Salathiel
19 42	130	-2126	Terah	49 12	*10*	-440	Zorobabel
20 41	100	-1996	**Abraham**	50 11	*40*	-401	Abiud
21 40	60	-1896	**Isaac**	51 10	*40*	-361	Eliakim
22 39	*81*	-1836	**Jacob**	52 9	*40*	-322	Azor
	Period 5&6 (Avg 66.0)			53 8	*40*	-282	Sadoc
23 38	*66*	-1755	Judas	54 7	*40*	-242	Achim
24 37	*66*	-1689	Phares	55 6	*40*	-203	Eliud
25 36	*66*	-1623	Esrom	56 5	*40*	-163	Eleazar
26 35	*66*	-1557	Aram	57 4	*40*	-124	Matthan
27 34	*66*	-1491	Aminadab	58 3	*40*	-84	Jacob
28 33	*66*	-1425	Naasson	59 2	*40*	-45	Joseph
29 32	*66*	-1359	Salman	60 1		-5	Jesus

Figures in italics created by Doddridge to facilitate averages resulting from Ussher data.
Period 1 average excludes Noah.
Ussher does not give an age for Jesse, except to quote a scripture saying he was old.

4h. Notable Differences.

Reviewing the greatest differences between the two chronologies is first the 264-year variance regarding the advent of Adam emerging from the Garden. For Ussher, Adam began his sojourn in 4004BC; for Doddridge it is 3740BC (4004-3740=264).

Second, for Ussher, Adam was in the Garden only hours. **"It is very probable, that Adam was turned out of paradise the same day that he was brought into it. ..."** For Doddridge, the time is unknown, whether for days, months or even years.

Third, Archbishop Ussher asserts that David was born 1085BC. This creates a dilemma, as when we begin to walk backwards from Ussher's 4004BC, we arrive at Ussher's stated birth of Jacob in 1836BC. Between Jacob and David are only 11 patriarchs. This leaves a whopping 751 years to the birth of David (1836-1085 = 751). And to make matters worse, the previous actual average birth-age for the Patriarchs had dropped to 31.4 years. But Ussher has only 11 patriarchs between Jacob and David, to spread out those 751 years (68.3-years average).
Next, Ussher puts the birth age for Jacob's son Judas (Judah) at 81 years (Doddridge at 83 years). While feasibly warranted, that decision conveniently used up some of the excess of the 751 years!
So, now Ussher has 10 patriarchs left in the remaining 670 year (751-81=670) spread, dropping the average to 67.0-years. This is still more than

double the preceding biblical history. Arbitrarily giving Jesse an extra 10 years to emphasize he was older than the average, we thereby drop the 67-year average to 66, with Jesse at 76.

Further, the resulting jump to a 66-year average for all of the patriarchs from Judas through Obed *(periods 5&6)* is somewhat high to defend, despite the Exodus, particularly after previous patriarchs from Arphaxad through Nahor were having their sons at a birth year average of 31.4 years *(periods 2&3 combined; period 3 had dropped even further from period 2, down to 30.25).*

The Doddridge Chronology first considered the Arphaxad-Nahor averages and then modified that base slightly higher at a 37.85-year average due to the more uneasy times between Judas and Obed, as shown in *period 5.*

Period 6 was even more stressful due to the Affliction and the Exodus. Doddridge arrived at a 59-year average for *period 6.*

This action resulted in David's birth coming in at 1035BC as opposed to Ussher's 1085BC.

The remaining balance of years, setting Jesus' birth at 5BC, creates a <40-year average for Ussher. Doddridge, for the same period, but with a 1AD birth for Jesus, calculates <38-year average.

5. Original Plan of the Gods

How many years were originally *planned* for the spirit sons and daughters of God for their mortal probation during the earth's temporal existence?

And the Gods prepared the waters that they might bring forth great whales, and every living creature that moveth, which the waters were to bring forth abundantly after their kind; and every winged fowl after their kind. And the Gods saw that they would be obeyed, and that **their plan was good**. *(Abr. 4:21, ba)*

And the Gods formed man from the dust of the ground, and took his spirit (that is, the man's spirit), and put it into him; and breathed into his nostrils the breath of life, and man became a living soul. *(Abr. 5:7)*

6. Q. What are we to understand by the book which John saw, which was sealed on the back with seven seals?

 A. We are to understand that it contains the revealed will, mysteries, and the works of God; the hidden things of his economy concerning this earth during **the seven thousand years of its continuance, or its temporal existence**. *(D&C 77:6; ba)*

12. Q. What are we to understand by the sounding of the trumpets, mentioned in the 8th chapter of Revelation?

 A. We are to understand that as God made the world in six days, and on the seventh day he finished his work, and sanctified it, and also formed man out of the dust of the earth, even so, **in the beginning of the seventh thousand years will the Lord God sanctify the earth, and complete the salvation of man**, and judge all things, and shall redeem all things, except that which he hath not put into his power, when he shall have sealed all things, unto the end of all things; and the sounding of the trumpets of the seven angels are the preparing and finishing of his work, in the beginning of the seventh thousand years—the preparing of the way before the time of his coming. *(D&C 77:12)*

These last two verses tell us there are 7,000 years planned for this mortal probationary state, with the last 1,000 years to be the sanctification or Millennial period to complete the salvation of man.

But before the Millennium, there is the 6,000-year mortal period (7,000 – 1,000 = 6,000) designed for us spirits to be born into mortality. At the end of the mortal probationary period comes the *Second* Coming of Jesus Christ who will then usher in the Millennium. The First Coming was in the Meridian of Time, the middle millennium in the plan, the plan of salvation.

> And now, behold, I say unto you: This is the plan of salvation unto all men, through the blood of mine Only Begotten, who shall come in **the meridian of time**. *(Moses 6:62; ba)*

The ushering in of the great and dreadful day of the Lord, the Second Coming, comes at the end of the mortal period.

> And Malachi, the prophet who testified of the coming of Elijah—of whom also Moroni spake to the Prophet Joseph Smith, declaring that he should come before the ushering in of the great and dreadful day of the Lord—were also there. *(D&C 138:46)*

33 So likewise ye, when ye shall see all these things, know that it is near, *even* at the doors.
34 Verily I say unto you, This generation *[in which these things shall be shown forth]* shall not pass, till all these things be fulfilled.
35 Heaven and earth shall pass away, but my words shall not pass away.
36 But of that day and hour knoweth no *man*, no, not the angels of heaven, but my Father only. *(Matt. 24:33-36; KJV; [JST] in brackets)*

If we consider that Adam was 130 years old, when he had Seth as his firstborn son, then we know that from Adam leaving the Garden of Eden and entering mortality to the birth of Seth, 130 years of the 6,000-year mortal period had passed away. Thus, the mortal habitation for the sons and daughters of God to be born as mortals on this earth was reduced by 130 years.

6,000 mortal years minus 130 years leaves us 5,870 remaining mortal years until the Second Coming of Christ and the onset of the Millennium (the seventh thousand years). And so, we can continue through the remaining 20 known number of patriarchs, whereby we know how old the father was when he had his firstborn son – from Adam down to Jacob. These 21 Patriarchs consumed 2,098 years of the 6,000-year period, 35% of the total.

Father's age at birth of the Patriarchal son

Gratefully, we can develop downward trends and averages provided to us by the 21 patriarchs, from 130 years (Adam-Seth) before begetting the patriarchal son down to 29 years (Nahor-Terah).

Other data such as how old Adam was when he died is irrelevant for this equation. What is important is to calculate a sensible father-to-firstborn average when the Scriptures do not give us that information. By adding up the knowns and the calculated unknowns, we can then establish a more accurate estimated depletion of the 6,000-year mortal period to date and then determine what years are likely left before the Millennium.

So, the **original** plan might have been 3500 years before Christ's birth + 3500 years afterwards (1830 years to the Restoration + 670 years to the end of Mortality [2500AD] + 1000-year Millennium = **7000 years**); + a guesstimated 70 years[24] Satan will be loosed *after* the Millennium, "a little season" (see Rev. 20:3 on p.83) = **7070 years**.

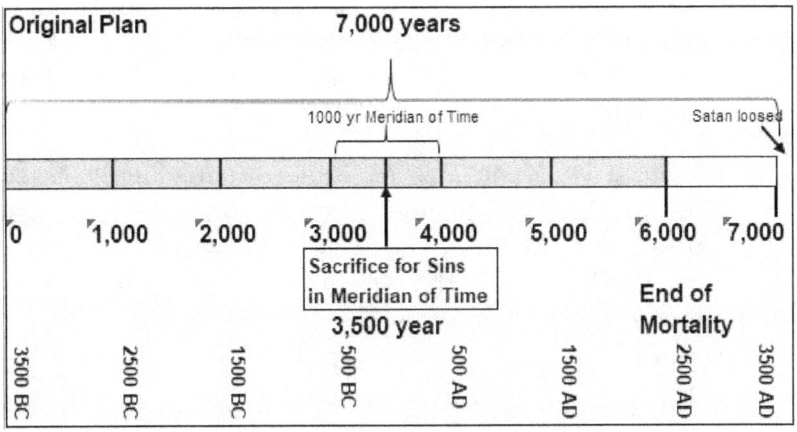

---

[24] 70-year *guesstimate* is derived by applying 1% of the 7,000-year temporal existence as a little season = 70 years

6. Modified Plan of the Gods

During the ensuing years following Adam's entrance into mortality, certain deviations from the original plan by the earth's inhabitants were observed by the Gods. While these developments were doubtless foreseen as alternate options by Them, Plan B was the new obvious course of action. **The Flood** was in the original plan of this 7,000-year span. The earth is to be resurrected for habitation by the children of God. Accordingly, the earth itself needed to be baptized. The Flood was the baptism. At the end of the mortal probation, it is to receive the gift of the Holy Ghost by fire, just like those who will reside upon it are to be converted, baptized and receive the gift of the Holy Ghost.

> And it came to pass when they were all baptized and had come up out of the water, the Holy Ghost did fall upon them, and they were filled with the Holy Ghost and with fire. *(3Nephi 19:13)*

> But the day of the Lord will come as a thief in the night; in the which the heavens shall pass away with a great noise, and the elements shall melt with fervent heat, the earth also and the works that are therein shall be burned up *(2 Pet. 3:10)*

Other things have transpired that were evidently not in the original plan. Regarding the horrors that the tribe of Judah committed to its own children:

> They have built also the high places of Baal, to burn their sons with fire *for* burnt offerings unto Baal, which I commanded not, nor spake *it*, **neither came *it* into my mind**: *(Jer. 19:5, same in JST; ba)*

And they built the high places of Baal, which *are* in the valley of the son of Hinnom, to cause their sons and their daughters to pass through *the* fire unto Molech; which I commanded them not, **neither came it into my mind**, that they should do this abomination, to cause Judah to sin. *(Jer. 32:35, same in JST; ba)*

Above, God clearly states that He did not intend the people of Judah would burn their own children to false gods. These verses show that things do happen that *may* cause God to adjust future plans.

Wherefore, I can stretch forth mine hands and hold all the creations which I have made; and mine eye can pierce them also, and among all the workmanship of mine hands there has not been so great wickedness as among thy brethren. *(Moses 7:36; among all the populated worlds in the universe, some of this earth's inhabitants are reputed as being the most wicked!)*

... the Jews... there is none other nation on earth that would crucify their God. *(2Ne10:3, written about 550BC, God did know beforehand how evil the Jews would be at the time of Christ – thus that was in the original plan. God populates the earth with the good, the lukewarm and the bad – with who, when, where and why, and adjusts as He sees fit (see Acts 17:26). But, God predicted that at the end of our mortal probation things would get so bad that a change in the plan was decided, perhaps made even from the pre-existence. See also D&C 124:49)*

21 For then shall be great tribulation, such as was not since the beginning of the world to this time, no, nor ever shall be.

22 And except those days should be shortened, there should no flesh be saved: but **for the elect's sake those days shall be shortened**. *(Matt. 24:21,22; ba)*

Therefore, God has decided to shorten the mortal probationary period. Shortened from what? From what was originally planned.

Operating by Faith.

God operates by knowledge for things present and past, and by faith for things future. Although God has all possible knowledge of things past and present, His works involving the future are accomplished by *faith*.

> 1 NOW faith is the substance of things hoped for, the evidence of things not seen. ...
>
> 3 **Through faith we understand that the worlds were framed by the word of God**, so that things which are seen were not made of things which do appear. *(Heb. 11:1,3; ba)*

If God knew everything in the future that would ever happen to the nth degree, then in reality the concept of agency would be destroyed, and all existence would be pre-determined. It would also imply there is an end to everything, since He would know everything there is to know right up to the last thing that will happen

> And God spake unto Moses, saying: Behold, I am the Lord God Almighty, and Endless is my name; for I am without beginning of days or end of years; and is not this endless? *(Moses 1:3; this verse apparently refers to God's eternal purposes of existence itself)*
>
> I am Alpha and Omega, the beginning and the end, the first and the last. *(Re. 22:13; this verse apparently refers to the pre-mortal and temporal existences of this earth)*

There is no end to everything, hence no end to the acquisition of new knowledge. Agency inherently contains an element of unpredictability, factored in all intelligent interaction. Agency produces *cause* for existence. If all existence was predetermined, then there would be no reason for existence to exist. Agency, or free will, really is the antonym to predetermination. If someone knows how something will end, then to the degree that he knows it, agency is absent.

18 Now I ask, is this faith? Behold, I say unto you, Nay; for **if a man knoweth a thing he hath no cause to believe, for he knoweth it.** ... 21 And now as I said concerning faith—**faith is not to have a perfect knowledge of things;** therefore if ye have faith ye hope for things which are not seen, which are true. *Alma 32:18, 21)*

14 **Through faith we understand that the worlds were framed** by the word of God: so that things which are seen were not made of things which do appear.

15 By this we understand that the principle of power, which existed in the bosom of God, by which the worlds were framed, was faith; and that it is by reason of this principle of power, existing in the Deity, that all created things exist – so that all things in heaven, on earth, or under the earth, exist by reason of faith, as it existed in HIM.

16 Had it not been for the principle of faith the worlds would never have been framed, neither would man have been formed of the dust – **it is the principle by which Jehovah works, and through which he exercises power over all temporal, as well as eternal things.** Take this principle or attribute, (for it is an attribute) from the Deity and he would cease to exist.

17 Who cannot see, that if **God framed the worlds by faith, that it is by faith that he exercises power over them,** and that faith is the principle of

power? And that if the principle of power, it must be so in man as well as in the Deity? This is the testimony of all the sacred writers, and the lesson which they have been endeavoring to teach to man. *(Lectures on Faith, Lecture First, 14-17, by Joseph Smith Jr; ba)*

Since God operates by faith, we can understand better when he spoke to Abraham through an angel, after he passed the test that God required of him:

> 10 And Abraham stretched forth his hand, and took the knife to slay his son.
>
> 11 And the angel of the LORD called unto him out of heaven, and said, Abraham, Abraham: and he said, Here *am* I.
>
> 12 And he said, Lay not thine hand upon the lad, neither do thou any thing unto him: **for now I know that thou fearest God,** seeing thou hast not withheld thy son, thine only *son* from me. *(Gen. 22:10-12; ba)*

Hence, God had *faith* that Abraham would actually follow through with the command to slay his son. Otherwise, the angel speaking for God would not have said "for NOW I know" after the fact.

And regarding Sodom and Gomorrah:

> 20 And the LORD said, Because the cry of Sodom and Gomorrah is great, and because their sin is very grievous;
>
> 21 **I will go down now, and see whether they have done** altogether according to the cry of it, which is come unto me; **and if not, I will know**. *(Gen. 18: 20,21; ba)*

We may conclude from verse 21 that once God learned what the two cities were up to, He would then only make His decisions regarding them.

Allowing the agency of man is the unknown variable wherein God exercises His faith, and then responds accordingly, adjusting His will as He deems it best. Joseph Smith taught:

> I teach them correct principles and they govern themselves." (*Messages of the First Presidency,* comp. James R. Clark, 6 vols., Salt Lake City: Bookcraft, 1965–75, 3:54.), *(taken from a talk by Elder Boyd K Packer, April 1990 General Conference)*

It may be reasoned that God works in the same manner. Through the Scriptures and the prophets, he teaches mankind "correct principles" and allows us our free will to govern ourselves accordingly.

Principle is defined as:

> a fundamental *[the foundation or basis of something]* truth or proposition that serves as the foundation for a system of belief or behavior or for a chain of reasoning; a general scientific theorem or law that has numerous special applications across a wide field. *(Google dictionary, viewed 18Mar2020)*

Much of the scriptures is devoted to providing us information about the times and lives of the prophets, all of which give life to those holy men and their deeds and may even be useful for our edification. But when it comes to the saving principles of exaltation?

> 1 THOUGH I speak with the tongues of men and of angels, and have not charity, I am become *as* sounding brass, or a tinkling cymbal.
> 2 And though I have *the gift of* prophecy, and understand all mysteries, and all knowledge; and though I have all faith, so that I could remove mountains, and have not charity, I am nothing.

3 And though I bestow all my goods to feed *the poor,* and though I give my body to be burned, and have not charity, it profiteth me nothing.

4 Charity suffereth long, *and* is kind; charity envieth not; charity vaunteth not itself, is not puffed up,

5 Doth not behave itself unseemly, seeketh not her own, is not easily provoked, thinketh no evil;

6 Rejoiceth not in iniquity, but rejoiceth in the truth;

7 Beareth all things, believeth all things, hopeth all things, endureth all things.

8 Charity never faileth: but whether *there be* prophecies, they shall fail; whether *there be* tongues, they shall cease; whether *there be* knowledge, it shall vanish away. ...

12 For now we see through a glass, darkly; but then face to face: now I know in part; but then shall I know even as also I am known.

13 And now abideth faith, hope, charity, these three; but the greatest of these *is* charity. *(1 Cor. 13:1-13)*

But the Scripture says God knows all things.

For if our heart condemn us, **God** is greater than our heart, and **knoweth all things**. *(1John 3:20; ba)*

And just a few chapters earlier John also said:

But ye have an unction* from the Holy One, **and ye know all things**. *(1 John 1:20; ba; *anointing)*

The common denominator with God and the anointed knowing all things is the Holy Spirit.

But the Comforter, *which is* the Holy Ghost, whom the Father will send in my name, he shall teach you **all things**, ... *(John 14:26; ba)*

The Second Coming.

Let us reckon that God feels the original plan needs to be shortened by 70 years (1% of the total temporal existence). Otherwise, all of the Elect will be destroyed in those days filled with tribulation from evil doers. This would modify the temporal 7,000-year period to 6,930 years and ***the mortal probation would end in the year 2190AD.***

So, the **modified** plan would be 3740 years before Christ's birth + 3190 years afterwards (1830 years to the Restoration of the Church + 360 years to the end of Mortality [= 2190AD] + 1000-year Millennium = **6930 years**); + 70 guesstimated years that Satan is to be loosed for a "little season" *after* the Millennium = **7000 years**).

The Apostle John explains this "little season:"

> 3 And cast him into the bottomless pit, and shut him up, and set a seal upon him, that he should deceive the nations no more, till the thousand years should be fulfilled: and after that **he must be loosed a little season**. ...
>
> 7 And **when the thousand years are expired**, Satan shall be loosed out of his prison,
>
> 8 And shall go out to deceive the nations which are in the four quarters of the earth, Gog and Magog, to gather them together to battle: the number of whom *is* as the sand of the sea.
>
> 9 And they went up on the breadth of the earth, and compassed the camp of the saints about, and the beloved city: and fire came down from God out of heaven, and devoured them.
>
> 10 And the devil that deceived them was cast into the lake of fire and brimstone, where the beast and the false prophet *are,* and shall be tormented day and night for ever and ever. *(Rev. 20:3, 7-10; ba)*

We can see that God has no intention of shortening or lengthening the 1,000-year millennial period. It can be moved up, but not made less.

Filling in the moved-up period from the 7,000-year plan, vacated *after* the end of the Millennium, will be a "little season" wherein Satan is to be loosed from prison to gather his armies for "the battle of the great God" (D&C 88:110-116), before this earth will become a new governing Celestial planet. Originally the little season was added on after the 7,000-year temporal existence, but now it is a part of it.

We can be confident that this period for Satan's last stand was in one way or another in the original plan, but perhaps as an addendum to the Millennium. The period for the loosening of Satan in this manner in the modified plan could likewise be a 70-year period, closing the gap that was created by shortening the mortal period, restoring in all the total original planned period of 7,000 years. But the idea here is that the shortening and the little season are about the same in time.

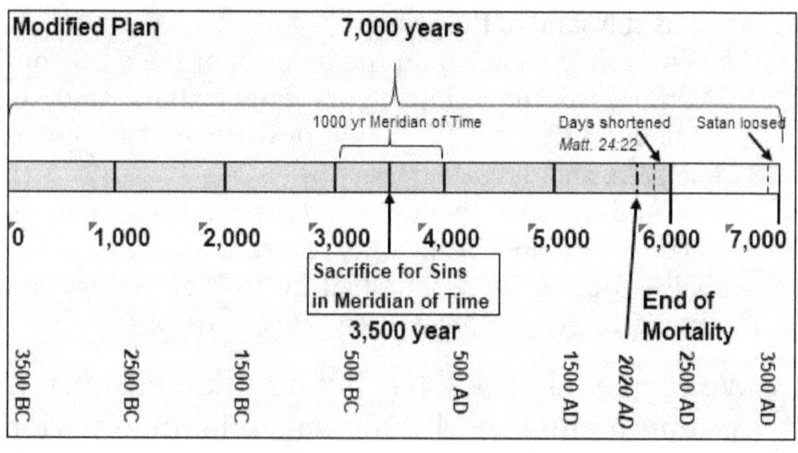

7. The 7,000 Year Temporal Existence

LIFE SPANS OF THE FIRST 22 PATRIARCHS

	THE FIRST TWENTY-TWO PATRIARCHS *(per JST)*				
	Birth Age	Patriarch	Death Age	Average Birth Age	Average Death Age
1	130	**Adam**	930	*Period 1*	
2	105	Seth	912		
3	90	Enos	905		
4	70	Cainan	910		
5	65	Mahalaleel	895	**115.6**	**881.0**
6	162	Jared	962	excl. Noah	
7	65	Enoch	*Did not die*		
8	187	Methusaleh	969		
9	182	Lamech	777		
10	**492**	**Noah** *	950		
11	100	Shem	600		
12	35	Arphaxad	438	*Period 2*	
13	30	Salah	433	**33.0**	**445.0**
14	34	Eber	464		
15	30	Peleg	239	*Period 3*	
16	32	Reu	239		**214.0**
17	30	Serug	230	**30.25**	
18	29	Nahor	148		
19	70	Terah *	205	*Period 4*	
20	**100**	**Abraham** *	175	**78.25***	**176.8**
21	60	Isaac *	180	excl. Jacob	
22	*83*	Jacob	147		

31.4 Avg.

Total **2,181** years - Adam to Jacob

* Noah, Terah, Abraham and Isaac experienced singular tumult and testing in their lives contributing to high birth ages (See Book of Abraham).

Note: Jacob birth age of having first-born son Judah at 83 years is estimated.

LIFE SPANS OF THE FIRST 22 PATRIARCHS

The above 22 Patriarchs chart and the Doddridge Chronology chart on p.68 show the patriarchs broken down into *periods 1* through *8*, and are placed to show the declension of average birth ages. Jacob's birth-age in *Period 4* is calculated only. *Period 7* is a hiccup with a scripture (1

Sam 17:12, see p.139) hinting that David was born to Jesse *possibly* in his old age. *Period 8* would be from Solomon to Joseph. Averages fill the unknown birth ages.

Notably, the lifespans of the first 11 Patriarchs were quite protracted, averaging 881 years (excluding Enoch), doubtless due to the slow amalgamation of mortal blood with their immortal fluids, inherited from their one-time fully immortal father Adam.

As previously quoted, the Book of Job records that man was **placed** on the earth, but the Book of Genesis records the following:

> 7 And the LORD God formed **man** *of* the dust of the ground, and breathed into his nostrils **the breath of life; and man became a living soul.**
>
> 8 And the LORD God planted a garden eastward in Eden; and **there he put the man whom he had formed**. *(Gen. 2:7, 8; ba; the Book of Genesis does not explain how or where this formation occurred, or whether or not it occurred on another earth; ba)*

Each earth begins with an Adam and an Eve.

> 33 And **worlds without number** have I created; and I also created them for mine own purpose; and by the Son I created them, which is mine Only Begotten.
>
> 34 And the first man of all men have I called **Adam, which is many**. *(Moses 1:33, 34; ba)*
>
> And Adam called his wife's name **Eve**, because she was the mother of all living; for thus have I, the Lord God, called the first of all women, **which are many**. *(Moses 4:26; ba)*

President Brigham Young also explained that the creation story as presented by Moses was a symbolic story.

> Well he [Adam] was made of the dust of the earth but not of this earth. He was made just the same way you and I are made but of another earth. ...

It is said by Moses the Historian that the Lord caused a deep sleep to come upon Adam and took from his side a rib and formed the woman that Adam called Eve – this should be interpreted that the man Adam, like all other men had the seed within him to propagate his species, but not the woman she conceives the seed but she does not produce it, consequently she was taken from the side or bowels of her father this explains the mystery of Moses' dark sayings in regard to Adam and Eve. *(Excerpts from the diary of L John Nuttall, personal secretary to President Brigham Young, John Taylor, and Wilford Woodruff. Source: LDS Church Archives, Ms/d/923/Leonard John Nuttall 1834-1905/ Wednesday Feb 07, 1877. Excerpts are from a talk Brigham Young; See also Scriptural References by Page at end of this book.)*

Brigham Young explained the process of immortal Adams becoming mortal (the immortal part does not become mortal, but rather mortality is "diffused" into the whole entity. When their mortal bodies finally succumb, the immortal part continues, just as with us. Our spirits do not decompose due to having lived a mortal life. But when we die, the still fully immortal spirit continues. Doubtless, the immortal bodies of all Adams likewise do not decompose but continue on.

After men have got their exaltations and their crowns – have become Gods, even the sons of God – are made Kings of kings and Lord of lords, they have the power then of propagating their species in spirit; and that is the first of their operations with regard to organizing a world.

Power is then given to them to organize the elements, and then commence the organization of tabernacles.

How can they do it? Have they to go to that earth? Yes, an Adam will have to go there, and he cannot do without Eve: he must have Eve to commence the work of generation, **and they will go into the garden, and continue to eat and drink of the fruits of the corporeal world, until this grosser matter is diffused sufficiently through their celestial bodies** to enable them, according to the established laws, to produce mortal tabernacles for their spiritual children. *(JD 6:274, 275, 28Aug1852; ba)*

Therefore, due to the slow process of diffusing mortality into immortal bodies, the first patriarchs had extra-long lives, they understandably waited for longer periods of time before having children so that their children would be *more* mortal. Otherwise, we might still be living our lives into the hundreds today. Is that bad? The plan calls for us spirits generally to be sufficiently tested in a life span of less than 120 years. God felt that was a suitable period of enough time for us to repent and establish our eternal priorities and direction.

We might guesstimate that when Adam left the Garden he was still 99.9% immortal. One piece of fruit is just a start. After 100 years of diffusing grosser, mortal matter, his newly acquired mortal body would then be pretty well along its way to completion and now he might have been only 85% immortal in all. Time to start having some kids. This is just guesswork to describe the process.

From Shem to Eber, mortality started having a greater dominating effect and lifespans began to spiral down dramatically. For this reason, I have broken down the period of the first twenty-two patriarchs into *four periods* (see chart on p85).

Finally, from Peleg to Jacob *(periods 3&4)*, the *lifespan* dropped to an average age of 195.4 years. Naturally, one might expect the average age of having their firstborn or patriarchal sons to drop likewise.

From Adam to Shem (less Noah), *the average birth-age* was 115.6 years *(Period 1)*. Bypassing Noah, who was an exception to the standard due no doubt to conditions before the Flood, from Arphaxad to Nahor the average birth-age *(Periods 2&3 combined)* dropped dramatically to 31.4 years

Again, this time skipping over Abraham, who was subjected to a series of tests from God including a longer period of time to wait to have his firstborn (a period similar in time to that of the earliest Patriarchs), we would expect a firstborn birth-year from Judas to Christ *(periods 5 and 8; see p68)* to return downwards approaching *periods 2 and 3*.

Now, during *period 8*, there was the scattering of Israel, numerous wars, etc. So, during that period the birth-age might have jumped up somewhat now and then, but generally we might expect the birth-year average to be closer to the 30s as in *periods 2&3* rather than in the 50s or 60s.

> 16 Therefore say, Thus saith the Lord GOD; Although I have cast them far off among the heathen, and although I have scattered them among the countries, yet will I be to them as a little sanctuary in the countries where they shall come.
>
> 17 Therefore say, Thus saith the Lord GOD; I will even gather you from the people, and assemble you out of the countries where ye have been scattered, and I will give you the land of Israel. *(Ezek.11:16,17)*

THE PATRIARCHS

#	Birth Year per Ussher	Birth Year per Doddridge	Patriarch	Age – first son per Ussher	Age – first son per Doddridge	Age at death p/Ussher	Age at death p/Dodd.	Death Year per Ussher	Death Year per Doddridge
1	−4004	−3740	Adam	130	130	930	930	−3074	−2810
2	−3874	−3610	Seth	105	105	912	912	−2962	−2698
3	−3769	−3505	Enos	90	90	905	905	−2864	−2600
4	−3679	−3415	Cainan	70	70	910	910	−2769	−2505
5	−3609	−3345	Mahalaleel	65	65	895	895	−2714	−2450
6	−3544	−3280	Jared	162	162	962	962	−2582	−2318
7	−3382	−3118	Enoch	65	65	365	430	−3017	−2688
8	−3317	−3053	Methuselah	187	187	969	969	−2349	−2084
9	−3130	−2866	Lamech	182	182	777	777	−2353	−2089
10	−2948	−2684	Noah *	502	492	950	950	−1998	−1734
11	−2446	−2192	Shem	100	100	600	600	−1846	−1592
12	−2346	−2092	Arphaxad	35	35	438	438	−1908	−1654
13	−2311	−2057	Salah	30	30	433	433	−1878	−1624
14	−2281	−2027	Eber	34	34	464	464	−1817	−1563
15	−2247	−1993	Peleg	30	30	239	239	−2008	−1754
16	−2217	−1963	Reu	32	32	239	239	−1978	−1724
17	−2185	−1931	Serug	30	30	230	230	−1955	−1701
18	−2155	−1901	Nahor	29	29	148	148	−2007	−1753
19	−2126	−1872	Terah	130	70	205	205	−1921	−1667
20	−1996	−1802	Abram	100	100	175	175	−1821	−1627
21	−1896	−1702	Isaac	60	60	180	180	−1716	−1522
22	−1836	−1642	Jacob	81	83	147	147	−1689	−1495
23	−1755	−1559	Judah				119		−1440

Total 2,249 2,181

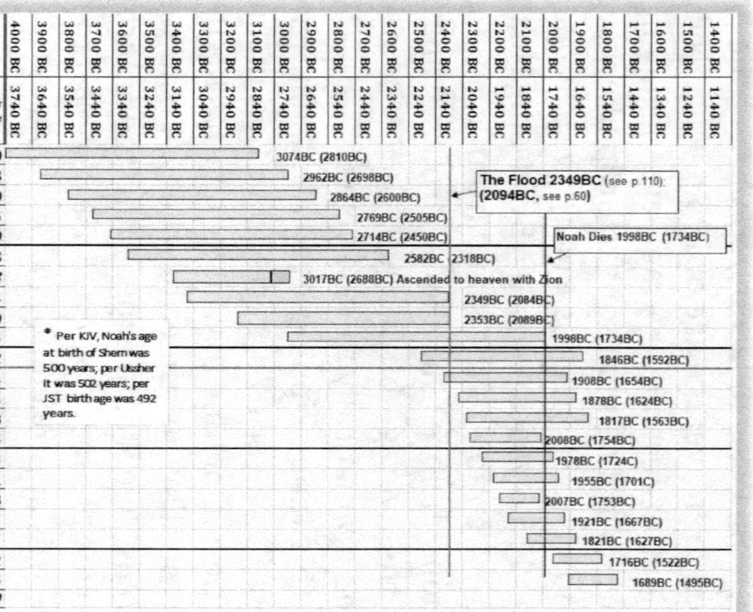

* KJV = King James Version (Gen. 5:32); JST = Joseph Smith Translation (Gen. 7:85).

Timeline axis (per Ussher / per Doddridge): 4000 BC / 3740 BC, 3900 BC / 3640 BC, 3800 BC / 3540 BC, 3700 BC / 3440 BC, 3600 BC / 3340 BC, 3500 BC / 3240 BC, 3400 BC / 3140 BC, 3300 BC / 3040 BC, 3200 BC / 2940 BC, 3100 BC / 2840 BC, 3000 BC / 2740 BC, 2900 BC / 2640 BC, 2800 BC / 2540 BC, 2700 BC / 2440 BC, 2600 BC / 2340 BC, 2500 BC / 2240 BC, 2400 BC / 2140 BC, 2300 BC / 2040 BC, 2200 BC / 1940 BC, 2100 BC / 1840 BC, 2000 BC / 1740 BC, 1900 BC / 1640 BC, 1800 BC / 1540 BC, 1700 BC / 1440 BC, 1600 BC / 1340 BC, 1500 BC / 1240 BC, 1400 BC / 1140 BC

Timeline bar end-labels:
3074BC (2810BC)
2962BC (2698BC)
2864BC (2600BC)
2769BC (2505BC)
2714BC (2450BC)
2582BC 2318BC)
3017BC (2688BC) Ascended to heaven with Zion
2349BC (2084BC)
2353BC (2089BC)
1998BC (1734BC)
1846BC (1592BC)
1908BC (1654BC)
1878BC (1624BC)
1817BC (1563BC)
2008BC (1754BC)
1978BC (1724C)
1955BC (1701C)
2007BC (1753BC)
1921BC (1667BC)
1821BC (1627BC)
1716BC (1522BC)
1689BC (1495BC)

The Flood 2349BC (see p.110); (2094BC, see p.60)

Noah Dies 1998BC (1734BC)

* Per KJV, Noah's age at birth of Shem was 500 years; per Ussher it was 502 years; per JST birth age was 492 years.

8. Orson Pratt Excerpts

Elder Orson Pratt (1811-1881) considered the scripture in the "Book of Covenants"[25] *(D&C 21:3)* and offered evidence its dating was to be a "present mode of reckoning" *(p95)* and not meant to establish the birth year of Christ, though he also disputed the accuracy of Ussher's Chronology. However, in the following excerpts he does address the date given in the Doctrine and Covenants *(see p.95; D&C 21:3)* which gives the statement that is often used to refer to Christ being born in 1AD.

---

[25] See p.95. The Book of Covenants in 1834, arranged by Sidney Rigdon and others, was later replaced with The Doctrine and Covenants in 1835. As Orson Pratt and others were still referring to it as the Book of Covenants in 1872, the name likely stuck as a shortened term for the Doctrine and Covenants.

*Revelation on Church Organization and Government, given through Joseph Smith the Prophet, **April 1830**. HC 1:64–70. Preceding his record of this revelation the Prophet wrote: "We obtained of him [Jesus Christ] the following, by the spirit of prophecy and revelation; which not only gave us much information, but also pointed out to us the precise day upon which, according to his will and commandment, we should proceed to organize his Church once more here upon the earth." ...*

1 THE rise of the Church of Christ in these last days, **being one thousand eight hundred and thirty years since the coming of our Lord and Savior Jesus Christ in the flesh,** it being regularly organized and established agreeable to the laws of our country, by the will and commandments of God, in the fourth month, and on the sixth day of the month which is called April— *(D&C 20:1; ba; see also p.65)*

*Revelation given to Joseph Smith the Prophet, at Fayette, New York, **April 6, 1830**. HC 1:74–79. This revelation was given at the organization of the Church, on the date named, in the home of Peter Whitmer, Sen. Six men, who had previously been baptized, participated. ...*

3 Which church was organized and established in the year of your Lord **eighteen hundred and thirty**, in the fourth month, and on the sixth day of the month which is called April. *(D&C 21:3; ba)*

Scriptures of the Church of **Jesus Christ** of Latter-day Saints cite the 92nd year of the reign of judges in America was 1AD, and it was then that Christ was born.

1 NOW it came to pass that **the ninety and first year had passed away** and it was six hundred years from the time that Lehi left Jerusalem; and it was in the year

that Lachoneus was the chief judge and the governor over the land. ...

11 And it came to pass that he went out and bowed himself down upon the earth, and cried mightily to his God in behalf of his people, yea, those who were about to be destroyed because of their faith in the tradition of their fathers.

12 And it came to pass that he cried mightily unto the Lord all that day; and behold, the voice of the Lord came unto him, saying:

13 Lift up your head and be of good cheer; for behold, **the time is at hand, and on this night shall the sign be given, and on the morrow come I into the world,** to show unto the world that I will fulfil all that which I have caused to be spoken by the mouth of my holy prophets. *(3 Nephi 1:1-13; ba)*

NOW it came to pass that the *ninety and first year had passed away and it was "six hundred years from the time that Lehi left Jerusalem; and it was in the year that ᵇLachoneus was the chief judge and the governor over the land.

[*A.D. 1]

(Book of Mormon, 3 Nephi 1:1)

Elder Orson Pratt states *(p96)* there are hundreds of chronologies trying to determine the age of the world that have been written, each disagreeing to some extent with one another. Suffice it to say, this book will go by D&C 20:1 and use the date 1AD for the birth of Christ. We are speaking of four years here, when we are trying to get to the nearest century. That said, I do not think we need to worry about the accuracy of 5BC or 1AD one way or the other. Now, on to some thoughts by Elder Pratt.

Journal of Discourses, Vol. 15, pp 261-263, 29Dec1872

261 There is another thing that, perhaps, a great many of the Latter–day Saints and many of the world have not reflected upon; that is, that the beginning of our present New Year is incorrect, reckoning the years from the birth of Christ, for the first day of January was not the day of his birth. We call it the first day of the year, but it has no reference to the day of Christ's birth. **The first day of the year of the true Christian era should be the day of the Savior's birth – the 11th day of April.** About 122 years ago we did not have the first day of January for New Year. At that time, or thereabouts, everybody in America and England reckoned New Year's Day on the 25th of March. That had been the first day of the year for many generations. How came it to be changed to the first day of January? In 1751 the Parliament of Great Britain passed a law that the year should be moved backwards from the 25th day of March to the 1st day of January, making the year 1751 some eighty–four days shorter than all the other years had been. Why did they do this? In order to place New year in connection with a certain event in astronomy. Those who are acquainted with the earth going round the sun, know that the path in which it moves is not a circle but an ellipse, or elongated circle. You make a wire into the form of a circle and then pull it out, and that is the form of an ellipse. The sun is situated in one of the foci of this ellipse, and is nearer to the earth on the 1st day of January or the 31st day of December, by about three millions of miles, than it is on the 1st day of July. The object of placing the year back was to have the year begin when the earth was in its perihelion in going around the sun. This was not the only alteration that has been made, but this accounts for the phrases "new style" and "old style," with which you occasionally meet in historical documents, the former having reference to the new mode of reckoning, the latter to the old mode.

I have said that this was not the only change made in time. In the year 1752 – when the second day of September had arrived, in order to bring the year to correspond with the seasons, it was found necessary to set the time forward so that the 3rd day of September should be called the 14th, eleven days being dropped out of the calendar. This was also established by parliamentary law; and in this way the seasons have been brought to correspond, in some measure, with the length of the year.

262 All these things should be taken into consideration in our dates; and when we read the saying in **the Book of Covenants**[26] that the Lord organized his Church in the year of our Lord 1830, in the fourth month, and on the sixth day of the month, **the Lord made his language to correspond with our present mode of reckoning**, that is, he adopted the reckoning of the English, established by parliamentary law. Instead of reckoning the year to begin on the 25th of March, he says, "It being in the year of our Lord 1830, the fourth month, and the sixth day of the month that the Church was organized." **We are not on this account to take this as the real date, but it is adapted to our present mode of reckoning**. I have made these remarks that no persons, if they should feel disposed to search into chronology, might be misled in relation to this matter. Being so near Christmas and New year, I have deemed it appropriate to dwell on this subject, for the purpose of enlightening the minds of all who may be present, so far as I have information in regard to it.

---

[26] Elder Orson Pratt is here referring to D&C 21:3. See p.92

Now, if I have not already occupied too much time, I desire to dwell a little upon the subject of the chronology of our world. We have no dates on which we can depend as to the period or history of our globe from the creation down to the present time. Chronologists differ in regard to the history and age of the world.

Some make the age of the world, from the creation to the coming of Christ, to be four thousand years. **Archbishop Usher*** has introduced this chronology into King James' Bible; and in that you will find all the dates adapted to that particular reckoning; and **according to his reckoning you will find that Christ came in the year of the world 4004. Is this to be depended upon? Not at all.** Many chronologists equally as learned, and who have made deeper researches than he has on this subject, differ with him materially. There are many who place the birth of Christ at 5500 years from the creation; others place it at 5490, others at 5508 or 9 years. **There are about two hundred chronologists who all differ in regard to this matter.** Many Jewish chronologists make it over six thousand years from the creation till the birth of Christ, so that you see when we attempt to take up the subject on the learning of the world, we are in the midst of confusion – no person knows anything about it. It is not really necessary that we should know, but we have some little light on this subject.

We know that it was not six thousand years from the creation to the birth of Christ. How do we know this? **God has told us in new revelation that this earth is destined to continue its temporal existence for seven thousand years**, and that at the commencement of the seventh thousand, he will cause seven angels to sound their trumpets. In other words, we may call it the Millennium, for the meaning of the word millennium is a thousand years. Six thousand years must pass away from the creation till the time that Jesus comes in the clouds of heaven, and he will not come exactly at the expiration of six thousand years. When the Prophet Joseph asked the Lord what was meant by the sounding of the seven trumpets, he was told, "That as God made the world in six days, and on the seventh day he finished his work and sanctified it, and also formed man out of the dust of the earth; even so in the beginning of the seventh thousand years, will the Lord God sanctify the earth, and complete the salvation of man, and judge all things and shall redeem all things, except that which he hath not put into his power when he shall have sealed all things unto the end of all things, and the sounding of the trumpets of the seven angels is the preparing and finishing of his work, in the beginning of the seventh thousand years; to prepare the way before the time of his coming." This quotation will be found in the Pearl of Great Price: 34.

263 Neither of these trumpets have sounded yet, but they shortly will; and this gives us a little clue to the period and age of our world. **We know that six thousand years have not yet elapsed since the creation, but we know that they have very nearly expired.** We know that God set up and established this kingdom 1800 years from the date of his crucifixion, preparatory to his coming in the clouds of heaven to receive the kingdom that he sets up here on the earth, and to rule and reign over all people, nations and tongues that are spared alive.

Journal of Discourses Vol. 16:317, 324, 325, 22Nov1873

317 These six days in which the Lord performed this work, I do not believe, were each limited to twenty–four hours, as are the periods which we now call day; indeed, when we come to new revelation, we find some light on this subject. In the Book of Abraham, as well as in the inspired translation of the Scriptures, given through Joseph Smith, the Lord says, in speaking of the work of creating this earth, that he was governed by celestial time. According to this new revelation, there is a certain great world, called Kolob, placed near one of the celestial kingdoms, whose diurnal rotation takes place once in a thousand of our years; and that celestial time was measured by those celestial beings, by the rotations of Kolob, hence one day with the Lord was a thousand of our years. If this was the case, the six days of the creation of our earth, the six days during which it was being prepared as a habitation for man, must have been six thousand of our years. When the Lord spoke to Adam, after having placed him in the Garden of Eden, concerning the forbidden fruit, saying – "In the day that thou eatest thereof thou shalt surely die!" we can not suppose that the day there referred to meant a day of twenty–four hours. It could not have meant that, for history informs us that Adam lived almost one thousand years from the time of the Fall; but before the day of a thousand years had wholly passed away his death did take place. ...

324 We are living, Latter–day Saints, near the close of the sixth thousand years from the fall of man; how near I do not know, and there is a great change about to take place. Inquires one – "Is there not some way by which we can fix the time, and arrive at a certainty in regard to the age of our globe since the fall of man?" I do not know of any way except by new revelation, for chronology is so imperfect that many hundreds who have spent their lives and fortunes in studying it, differ from each other in their conclusions. One has one date for the age of the world, and another has another. Let me give to you a few specimens. We will take one of the oldest eras – the Alexandrian – computed by Julius Africanus. In this Alexandrian era, the time from the creation to the birth of Christ is set down at 5,500 years; in the Antioch era, computed by Pannorus, it is set down at 5,493 years; in the Constantinople, or Greek era, it is set down at 5,509 years; you take Scaliger, another great chronologist, and he, by a comparison of the text of various ancient manuscripts, makes the age of the world, from the creation to the coming of Christ, 3,950 years. Then you take another celebrated man, Father Pezron, and he makes it 5,873 years from the creation to Christ. Then you take the one who has given the chronology to the Bible, Archbishop Usher*, and he makes it 4,004 years from the creation to Christ. Another chronologist, Josephus, makes it 4,163 years; and you take some other Jewish chronologists, and they make it as high as 6,524 years from the creation to Christ. How are you going to judge? You may take over two hundred other chronologists, whose names are given, and they all have their special dates; consequently, you see, we are utterly at a loss, and without new revelation, we are no more sure that Archbishop Usher's* chronology, contained in King James's Bible, is correct, than we have to suppose that that many of those others are correct. What shall we do, then? The best thing for us to do is to depend upon what God reveals. If he gives us any knowledge regarding chronology, depend upon it; and he has given us a great deal of information with regard to the signs of the times. If he has not given us the age of the world, he has given us that whereby we may know that we live in the generation in which the times of the Gentiles will be fulfilled. ... And then we have other revelations, showing that when their times are fulfilled there is a speedy and short work to be accomplished in the gathering of the house of Israel from the four quarters of the earth. They are to be brought out of all nations, kindreds, tongues, and people with a mighty hand and outstretched arm. We are told that God will then perform wonders, miracles and signs, greater than ever have been performed since the creation of the world; that he will bring back his covenant people. ...

325 After the Jews have rebuilt Jerusalem, and after the Temple is erected, the Lord Jesus will come.

A Series of Pamphlets, the Great First Cause, p.4,5
Printed by R. James, Liverpool, 1851

4... Light does not inform us whether the most distant luminous bodies which can be seen are now in existence or not. Light enables us to see them exist thousands of ages ago, but it gives us no indications that they have existed as luminous bodies since that period.

If the light of all worlds were created only six thousand years ago, then it would be impossible to see any of them over thirty-seven thousand billions of miles distant; for light could not travel over that distance in six thousand years: all beyond that would be invisible, and remain so, until their light had time to reach us. ...

5 Now, can we, for one moment suppose that within the comparatively little regions, occupied by our stellar universe, no light existed until six thousand years ago, when we are almost irresistibly compelled to admit that there previously existed in the infinite regions beyond a vast immense ocean of luminiferous fluid?

We can come to no other conclusion, but that worlds, and systems of worlds, and universes of worlds existed in the boundless heights and depths of immensity before the foundations of our ancient earth were laid.

(Ddd note: "Ussher" misspelled in JD as "Usher"; quoted here 3x)

9. Ussher Chronology

The following excerpts are extracted from Ussher's Chronology as available freely from several web sites *in pdf format* (see Bibliography section of this book). It can also be obtained from eBay sources as well as in hard copy book form. This primary pdf copy has a number of typos, etc. that I did not correct, as they are inconsequential.

The hard copy book version (960 pages) differs significantly here and there from the pdf versions used for this book. Notably, 1762d … 2242BC is missing in most of the pdf forms I reviewed. That would have been number 49, and number 50 would be 1771a … 2234BC. As this download here is from a specific pdf copy, I decided to leave it as is, except that I added the brief 2242BC as it appears in a few of online pdf sources as well as the hard copy. As most pdf versions I viewed made the same exclusion, I made the decision not to change all of the numbering thereafter. Hence, in this rendition there are two number 50s; otherwise the numbering follows the pdf version.
A few entries from the pdf version were made also regarding the birth of Christ in the Annals. Noteworthy is the numbering again. 6057 in the primary pdf is 6059 in the hard copy, indicating another glitch between the pdf and the hard copy.

Note: I have added emphasis (bold font) to some of Ussher's text to facilitate reading the material.
There is no intent to annotate this section. Nevertheless, a few minor corrections and clarifications were made.

{d} and {e} on pp.102-104 are quoted from an inserted section into the Annals, between The Epistle … and The First Age …, titled "Explanatory Notes by Editor," in two of several pdf copies I searched. The section is also found in the hard copy.

The Annals of The World
by
Rev. James Ussher
LONDON,
Printed by E. Tyler, for F. Crook, and G. Bedell 1658

...

The Epistle to the Reader   ...

(Ddd Note: this location is in the hard copy version, p10)

I used the following abbreviations:

AD Years from the start of the Christian era.

AM Year of the World from creation.

BC Years before the Christian era.

JP Julian Year starting at January 1, 4713 BC.

NK Northern Kingdom of Israel.

SK Southern Kingdom of Israel.

After the time denoted by AM, one of four letters may be affixed.

a Autumn

b Winter

c Spring

d Summer

Other things the prudent reader will figure out for himself. I wish you the enjoyment of these endeavours and bid you farewell.

London, July 13, 1650 AD.

Rev. James Ussher

Explanatory Notes by Editor   ...

{d} Time of Creation

Since the Jews used to start their year in the autumn, this is not an unreasonable assumption.

Also the biblical pattern of "evening and morning" seems to apply to year as well as days. First the dark months of autumn and winter and then the bright months of spring and summer. This also fits the biblical pattern in spiritual matters too. For the saint, his worst lot in life comes first followed by an eternal day of happiness in Christ. The best wine comes last. Joh 2:10 See Spurgeon's Sermon No. 225, "Satan's Banquet" and No. 226, "The Feast of the Lord".

{e} The Christian Era

The Christian Era should properly beg[i]n with the year Christ was born; and in devising it, the intention was to have it begin with that year. By the "Christian Era" is meant the system upon which calendars are constructed and by which historical events are now dated in practically all the civilized world. But the originator of the system made a miscalculation as to the year (in the calendar then in use) in which Christ was born, as the result of which the year A.D. 1 was fixed four years too late. **In other words, the Lord Jesus was four years old in the year A.D. 1.**

The mistake came about in this way: The Christian Era (i.e. the scheme of dates beginning A.D.1) was not devised until A.D. 532. Its inventor, or contriver, was a monk named Dionysius Exiguus. At that time the system of dates in common use began from the era of the emperor Diocletian, A.D. 284. Exiguus was not willing to connect his system of dates with the name of that infamous tyrant and persecutor. So he conceived the idea of connecting his system with and dating all its events from, the Incarnation of Jesus Christ. His reason for wishing to do this was, as he wrote to Bishop Petronius, "to the end that the commencement of our hope might be better known to us and that the cause of man's restoration, namely, our Redeemer's passion, might appear with clearer evidence."

For the carrying out of this excellent plan, it was necessary to fix the date of the Incarnation in the terms of the chronological systems then in vogue. The Romans dated the beginning of their history from the supposed date of the founding of the city ("ab urbe condita" or A.U.C as usually abbreviated). Dionysius Exiguus calculated that the year of our Lord's birth was A.U.C. 753. He made his equivalence of dates from Lu 3:1, "Now in the fifteenth year of the reign of Tiberius Caesar" etc., at which time Christ was 30 years of

age according to Lu 3:23. But it was ascertained later that a mistake of four years had been made; for it clearly appears by Mt 2:1 that Christ was born before the death of Herod, who died in 749 A.U.C. Tiberius succeeded Augustus, Aug. 19, A.U.C. 767. Hence his 15th year would be A.U.C. 779; and from those facts Dionysius was right in his calculation. But it was discovered in later years that Tiberius began to reign as colleague with Augustus four years before the latter died [27]. Hence the 15th year mentioned by Luke was four years earlier than was supposed by Dionysius and consequently the birth of Christ was that many years earlier than the date selected by Exiguus, which date has been followed ever since. This must be allowed for in any computation of dates which involves events happening before Christ.
"The Wonders of Bible Chronology", Page[s] 84,85, Philip Mauro [1859-1952], first published 1922, Reprinted by, Reiner Publications, Swengel, Pennsylvania

...

The First Age of the World

1a AM, 710JP, **4004 BC**
1. In the beginning God created the heaven and the earth. Ge 1:1 **This beginning of time**, according to our chronology, happened at **the start of the evening preceding the 23rd day of October in the year of the Julian calendar, 710**

2. **On the first day** Ge 1:1-5 of the world, on Sunday, October 23rd, God created the highest heaven and the angels. When he finished, as it were, the roof of this building, he started with the foundation of this wonderful fabric of the world. He fashioned this lower most globe, consisting of the deep and

---

[27] Tiberius was born Tiberius Claudius Nero, later name changed to Tiberius Caesar Augustus or Tiberius Julius Caesar Augustus. Lived 42BC – 37AD. Period of reign is regarded to have begun in 14AD. (https://www.ancient.eu/Tiberius/; *excerpt viewed 12Dec2019*).

of the earth. Therefore, all the choir of angels sang together and magnified his name. Job 38:7 When the earth was without form and void and darkness covered the face of the deep, God created light on the very middle of the first day. God divided this from the darkness and called the one "day" and the other "night".

3. **On the second day** Ge 1:6-8 (Monday, October 24th) after the firmament or heaven was finished, the waters above were separated from the waters here below enclosing the earth.

4. **On the third day** Ge 1:9-13 (Tuesday, October 25th) when these waters below ran together into one place, the dry land appeared. From this collection of the waters God made a sea, sending out from here the rivers, which were to return there again. Ec 1:7 He caused the earth to bud and bring forth all kinds of herbs and plants with seeds and fruits. Most importantly, he enriched the garden of Eden with plants, for among them grew the tree of life and the tree of knowledge of good and evil. Ge 2:8,9

5. **On the fourth day** (Wednesday, October 26th) the sun, the moon and the rest of the stars were created.

6. **On the fifth day** (Thursday, October 27th) fish and flying birds were created and commanded to multiply and fill the sea and the earth.

7. **On the sixth day** (Friday, October 28th) the living creatures of the earth were created as well as the creeping creatures. Last of all, man was created after the image of God, which consisted principally in the divine knowledge of the mind, Col 3:10 in the natural and proper sanctity of his will. Eph 4:24 When all living creatures by the divine power were brought before him, Adam gave them their names. Among all of these, he found no one to help him like himself. Lest he

should be destitute of a suitable companion, God took a rib out of his side while he slept and fashioned it into a woman. He gave her to him for a wife, establishing by it the law of marriage between them. He blessed them and bade them to be fruitful and multiply. God gave them dominion over all living creatures. God provided a large portion of food and sustenance for them to live on. To conclude, because sin had not yet entered into the world, God saw every thing that he had made, and, behold, it was very good. And the evening and the morning were the sixth day. Ge 1:31

8. Now **on the seventh day**, (Saturday, October 29th) when God had finished his work which he intended, he then rested from all labour. He blessed the seventh day and ordained and consecrated the sabbath Ge 2:2,3 because he rested on it Ex 31:17 and refreshed himself. Nor as yet (for ought appears) had sin entered into the world. Nor was there any punishment given by God, either upon mankind, or upon angels. Hence is was, that this day was set forth for a sign, as well as for our sanctification in this world Ex 31:13 of that eternal sabbath, to be enjoyed in the world to come. In it we expect a full deliverance from sin and its dregs and all its punishments. Heb 4:4,9,10

9. **After the first week of the world ended, it seems that God brought the newly married couple into the garden of Eden.** He charged them not to eat of the tree of knowledge of good and evil but left them free to eat of everything else.

10. The Devil envied God's honour and man's obedience. He tempted the woman to sin by the serpent. By this he got the name and title of the old serpent. Re 12:9 20:2 The woman was beguiled by the serpent and the man seduced by the woman. They broke the command of God concerning the forbidden fruit. Accordingly when sought for by God and convicted of this crime, each had their punishments

imposed on them. This promise was also given that the seed of the woman should one day break the serpent's head. Christ, in the fulness of time should undo the works of the Devil. 1Jo 3:8 Ro 16:20 Adam first called her Eve because she was then ordained to be the mother, not only of all that should live this natural life, but, of those also who should live by faith in her seed. This was the promised Messiah as Sarah also later was called the mother of the faithful. 1Pe 3:6 Ga 4:31.

(Ddd note: This location is in hard copy version, p18)
11. After this our first parents were clothed by God with raiment of skins. They were expelled from Eden and a fiery flaming sword set to keep the way leading to the tree of life so that they should never eat of that fruit which they had not yet touched. Ge 3:21,22 **It is very probable, that Adam was turned out of paradise the same day that he was brought into it.** This seems to have been on the 10th day of the world. (November 1st) On this day also, in remembrance of so remarkable an event the day of atonement was appointed Le 23:27, and the yearly fast, spoken of by Paul, Ac 27:9 termed more especially by the name of nhsteian. On this feast all, strangers as well as native Israelites, were commanded to afflict their souls that every soul which should not afflict itself upon that day should be destroyed from among his people, Le 16:29 23:29

12. After the fall of Adam, **Cain** was the first of all mortal men that was born of a woman. Ge 4:1

130d AM, 840 JP, **3874 BC**
13. When Cain, the firstborn of all mankind, murdered Abel, God gave Eve another son called **Seth**. Ge 4:25 **Adam had now lived 130 years**. Ge 5:3 From whence it is gathered, that between the death of Abel and the birth of Seth, there was no other son born to Eve. For then, he should have been

recorded to have been given her instead of him. Since man had been on the earth 128 years and Adam and Eve had other sons and daughters Ge 5:4 the number of people on the earth at the time of this murder could have been as many as 500,000. Cain might justly fear, through the conscience of his crime, that every man that met him would also slay him. Ge 4:14,15

235d AM, 945 JP, **3769 BC**
14. When Seth was 105 years old, he had his son, **Enos**. This indicates the lamentable condition of all mankind. For even then was the worship of God wretchedly corrupted by the race of Cain. Hence it came, that men were even then so distinguished, that they who persisted in the true worship of God, were known by the name of the children of God. They who forsook him, were termed the children of men. Ge 4:26 6:1,2

325d AM, 1035 JP, **3679 BC**
15. **Cainan, the son of Enos was born** when his father was 90 years old. Ge 5:10

395d AM, 1105 JP, **3609 BC**
16. **Mahalaleel was born** when Cainan his father was 70 years old. Ge 5:12

460d AM, 1170 JP, **3544 BC**
17. **Jared was born** when his father Mahalaleel was 65 years old. Ge 5:15

622d AM, 1332 JP, **3382 BC**
18. **Enoch was born** when his father Jared was 162 years old. Ge 5:18

687d AM, 1397 JP, **3317 BC**
19. **Methuselah was born** when Enoch his father was 65 years old. Ge 5:25

874d AM, 1584 JP, **3130 BC**
20. **Lamech was born** when his father Methuselah was 187 years old. Ge 5:25

930d AM, 1640 JP, 3074 BC
21. Adam, the first father of all mankind, died at the age of 930 years. Ge 5:5

987d AM, 1697 JP, 3017 BC
22. Enoch, the 7th from Adam at the age of 365 years, was translated by God in an instant, while he was walking with him that he should not see death. Ge 5:23,24 Heb 11:5

1042d AM, 1752 JP, 2962 BC
23. Seth, the son of Adam died when he was 912 years old. Ge 5:8

1056d AM, 1766 JP, **2948 BC**
24. **Noah, the 10th from Adam, was born** when his father Lamech was 182 years old. Ge 5:29

1140d AM, 1850 JP, 2864 BC
25. Enos, the 3rd from Adam, died when he was 905 years old. Ge 5:11

1235d AM, 1945 JP, 2769 BC
26. Cainan, the 4th from Adam, died when he was 910 years old. Ge 5:14

1290d AM, 2000 JP, 2714 BC
27. Mahalaleel, the 5th from Adam, died when he was 892 years old. Ge 5:17

1422d AM, 2132 JP, 2582 BC
28. Jared, the 6th from Adam, died when he was 962 years old. Ge 5:20

1536a AM, 2245 JP, 2469 BC
29. Before the deluge of waters upon the whole wicked world, God sent Noah, a preacher of righteousness to them, giving them 120 years to repent of their evil ways. 1Pe 3:20 2Pe 2:5 Ge 6:3

1556d AM, 2266 JP, **2448 BC**
30. **Noah** was 500 years old when his 1st son, **Japheth** was born. Ge 5:32 10:21

1558d AM, 2268 JP, **2446 BC**
31. **Noah's 2nd son, Shem, was born 2 years later because 2 years after the flood, Shem was 100 years old.** Ge 11:10

1651d AM, 2361 JP, 2353 BC
32. Lamech, the 9th from Adam, died when he was 777 years old. Ge 5:31

1656a AM, 2365 JP, **2349 BC**
33. **Methuselah**, the 8th from Adam, **died** when he was 969 years old. He lived the longest of all men yet died before his father. Ge 5:27,24

34. Now in the 10th day of the second month of this year (Sunday, November 30th) God commanded Noah that in that week he should prepare to enter into the Ark. Meanwhile the world, totally devoid of all fear, sat eating and drinking and marrying and giving in marriage. Ge 7:1,4,10 Mt 24:38

35. In the 600th year of the life of Noah, on the 17th day of the second month, (Sunday, December 7th), **he with his children and living creatures of all kinds had entered into the Ark**. God sent a rain on the earth 40 days and 40 nights. The waters continued upon the earth 150 days, Ge 7:4,6,11-13,17,24.

36. The waters abated until the 17th day of the 7th month, (Wednesday, May 6th) when the ark came to rest upon one of the mountains of Ararat. Ge 8:3,4

37. The waters continued receding until on the 1st day of the 10th month (Sunday, July 19th) the tops of the mountains were seen. Ge 8:5

38. After 40 days, that is on the 11th day of the 11th month (Friday, August 28th) Noah opened the window of the ark and sent forth a raven. Ge 8:6,7

39. 7 days later, on the 18th day of the 11th month (Friday, September 4th) as may be deduced from the other 7 days mentioned in Ge 8:10, Noah sent out a dove. She returned after 7 days.
25th day of the 11th month, (Friday, September 11th) He sent her out again and about the evening she returned bringing the leaf of an olive tree in her bill. After waiting 7 days more, 2nd day of the 12th month, (Friday, September 18th) he sent the same dove out again, which never returned. (Ge 8:8,12)

The Second Age of the World

1657a AM, 2366 JP, 2348 BC
40. When Noah was 601 years old, on the 1st day of the 1st month (Friday, October 23rd), the 1st day of the new post-flood world, the surface of the earth was now all dry. Noah took off the covering of the ark. Ge 8:13

41. On the 27th of the 2nd month, (Thursday, December 18th) the earth was entirely dry. By the command of God, Noah went forth with all that were with him in the ark. Ge 8:14,15,19

42. When he left the ark, Noah offered to God sacrifices for his blessed preservation. God restored the nature of things destroyed by the flood. He permitted men to eat flesh for their food and gave the rainbow for a sign of the covenant which he then made with man. Ge 8:15-9:17

43. **Man's lifespan was now half the length it was previously.**

1658d AM, 2368 JP, **2346 BC**
44. **Arphaxad, was born to Shem when he was 100 years old**, 2 years after the flood. Ge 11:10

1693d AM, 2403 JP, **2311 BC**
45. **Salah was born**, when his father Arphaxad was 35 years old. Ge 11:12

1723d AM, 2433 JP, **2281 BC**
46. **Eber was born**, when Salah his father was 30 years old. Ge 11:14

1757d AM, 2467 JP, **2247 BC**
47. **When Eber was 34 years old, Peleg his son was born.** Ge 11:16 He called him Peleg for in his days the earth was divided. Ge 10:25 1Ch 1:19 If this happened at the day of his birth, then it seems that when Peleg was born, Noah, who formerly knew all the places which were now covered with bushes and thorns, divided the land among his grandchildren. When this was done, they then went from those eastern parts (where they first went from the mountains of Ararat) into the valley of Shinar. Ge 11:2 Here the people impiously conspired as we find in the book of Wisdom /APC Wis 10:5 to hinder this dispersion of them as commanded by God and began by Noah (as may be gathered from Ge 11:4,6,8,9 compared together). They went together to build the city and tower of Babylon. God frustrated this project by the confusion of languages he sent among them. (Hence it took the name of Babel Ge 11:9). The dispersion of

nations followed. Many companies and colonies settled down in various places according to their languages. The 13 sons of Joktan, the brother[s] of Peleg, as recorded in Ge 10:26-30 were among the captains and heads of the various companies. These brothers were not yet born when Peleg was born. Eber was only 34 years old when Peleg was born to him. Though we should suppose that Joktan was born, when Eber was only 20 years of age and that Joktan's oldest son was born to him when he was likewise 20 years old, yet still it appears, that the oldest son of Joktan must be 6 years younger than Peleg. So that at least the youngest of those 13 sons of Joktan, namely, Jobab and 3 other brothers of his are mentioned before him must be younger still. These countries rich in gold, Sheba, Ps 72:15 Ophir 1Ki 9:28 and Havilah Ge 2:11 were named after these men.

These brothers could not be capable of such an expedition of leading colonies because of their youth until some years after Reu was born to Peleg.

(Ddd note: "the brothers of Peleg" should be in the singular)

48. Man's lifespan was now a quarter of the length it was before the flood.

(Ddd note: this 1762d entry is not in many of the pdf copies)

1762d AM, 2472 JP, **2242 BC**

49. The **Tower of Babel** happened five years after the birth of Peleg, according to Georgius Syncellus' translation of the Book of Sothis. {*Manetho, Book of Sothis, l.1.1:239*}

(Ddd note: thus, Noah was 696 years old at the time of Babel, if this deduction by Syncellus' is correct [Doddridge: 2684BC– (1993BC–5) = 696; Ussher: 2948BC-(2247-5) = 706]. It also implies that the Patriarch Noah may have left the Tower along with Jared[28] and his family and friends, to return to his birthplace in what is now Missouri in America.

1771a AM, 2480 JP, 2234 BC

50. 1903 years elapsed from this time to the capture of Babylon by Alexander the Great. This calculation and

---

[28] See the Book of Ether in the Book of Mormon.

number of years was made according to astronomical observations by Porphyry, as we find in Simplicius, in his second book "de Coelo". This he affirms to have been transmitted into Greece from Babylon by Chalisthenes at Aristotle's request. From these writings it appears that the Babylonians devoted themselves to the study of astronomy, even from the very days of Nimrod, from whom all that region took the name of the land of Nimrod. Mic 5:6 Nimrod built Babylon and was the instigator of the building of the tower of Babel according to Josephus (l. 1. Antiq. c. 4.) Moses affirms that the royal seat of that kingdom was here. Ge 10:10 Nimrod made Babylon famous in those days. Jer 5:15 (See note on 3674a <<1898>>)

1787d AM, 2497 JP, **2217 BC**
50. **Reu or Ragau, was born when Peleg his father was 30 years old**. Ge 11:18

1816d AM, 2526 JP, 2188 BC
51. Constantinus Manasses states that the Egyptian state lasted 1663 years. Counting backward from the time that Cambyses, king of Persia, conquered Egypt, leads us to this period. About this time Mizraim, the son of Ham, led his colony into Egypt. Hence Egypt was called sometimes the land of Mizraim, sometimes of Ham, Ps 105:23,27 106:21,22 From this it was that the Pharisees later boasted that they were the sons of ancient kings. /APC Es 16:11 (See note on 3479b AM <<988>>)

1819d AM, 2529 JP, **2185 BC**
52. **Serug** or Saruch, **was born** when Ragau was 32 years old. Ge 11:20

1849d AM, 2559 JP, **2155 BC**
53. **Nachor was born** when Saruch his father was 30 years old. Ge 11:22

1878d AM, 2588 JP, **2126 BC**
54. **Terah** or Thara **was born** when Nachor his father was 29 years old. Ge 11:24

1915c AM, 2625 JP, 2089 BC
55. At this time Egialeus, king of the Sicyonians, in Peloponesus began his reign, 1313 years before the first olympiad. (Euseb. Chron.)

1920c AM, 2630 JP, 2084 BC
56. A people from Arabia bordering upon Egypt, called by the Egyptians Hyksos, meaning "kingly shepherds", invaded Egypt. They took Memphis and took over all of lower Egypt that bordered upon the Mediterranean Sea. Salatis, their 1st king, reigned 19 years, according to Josephus in his 1st book "cont. appiencem" as from Manetho.

1939c AM, 2649 JP, 2065 BC
57. Bnon, their 2nd king, reigned for 44 years, {*Manetho, 1:83}

1948d AM, 2658 JP, **2056 BC**
58. **When Terah was 70 years old, his oldest of three sons, Haran was born. Ge 11:26 Abram was not born for another 60 years as we shall see later.** Haran was the father-in-law later of the 3rd brother Nachor. For this man died before his father Terah left Ur of the Chaldeans and left a daughter named Milcah, who was married to his uncle Nachor, Ge 11:28,29

1983c AM, 2693 JP, 2021 BC
59. At this time Apachnan reigned in Egypt for 36 years and 7 months. {*Manetho, 1:83}

1996d AM, 2706 JP, 2008 BC
60. Peleg the 6th from Noah, died 209 years after the birth of Ragau. Ge 11:19

1997d AM, 2707 JP, 2007 BC
61. Nachor the 9th from Noah, died 119 years after the birth of his son Terah. Ge 11:25

2006d AM, 2716 JP, **1998 BC**
62. **Noah, died** when he had lived 950 years, 350 years after the deluge. Ge 9:28,29

2008c AM, 2718 JP, **1996 BC**
63. **Abram was born.** He was 75 years old when Terah his father died at the age of 205 years. Ge 11:32 12:1, 4 Ac 7:4 *(Ddd note: see notes on page 156)*

2018c AM, 2728 JP, 1986 BC
64. Sarai, who is also called Iscah the daughter of Haran, Ge 11:29,30, was born and was 10 years younger than her husband Abraham. Ge 17:17

2020b AM, 2730 JP, 1984 BC
65. Apophis reigned in Egypt for 61 years. {*Manetho, 1:83}

2026d AM, 2736 JP, 1978 BC
66. Reu or Ragau the 7th from Noah, died 207 years after the birth of Serug. Ge 11:21

2049d AM, 2759 JP, 1955 BC
67. Serug or Saruch, the 8th from Noah, died 200 years after the death of Nachor. Ge 11:23

2079b AM, 2789 JP, 1925 BC
68. About this time, Chedorlaomer king of Elam, or Elimais, situated between Persia and Babylon, conquered the kings of Pentapolis, Sodom, Gomorrah, Adma, Zeboiim and Bela, or Zoar. These served him 12 years. Ge 14:1,2,4

2081b AM, 2791 JP, 1923 BC
69. Jannas reigned in Egypt for 50 years and one month. {*Manetho, 1:83}

2083a AM, 2792 JP, 1922 BC

70. God called Abraham out of Ur, of the Chaldeans, to go into the land that he would show him. Ge 15:7 Jos 24:2,3 Ne 9:7 Ac 7:2-4. Ur was located in Mesopotamia according to Stephen the first martyr and Abarbenel. Ge 11:1-32 Ur was the city of the priests and mathematicians, who from their art, were called by the name of Chaldeans. By this name also even in Chaldea itself, those Genethliaci, or recorders of genealogies were distinguished and known from the rest of the Magi or wise men of that country, as we find in Da 2:2,10 4:7 5:11. These taught Terah and his sons idolatry. Jos 24:2 Terah therefore took Abram his son and Lot his nephew, the son of Haran and Sarai his daughter-in-law, Abram's wife, and started their journey together from Ur of the Chaldeans, to go into the land of Canaan. They came to Haran in the same country of Mesopotamia and there they stayed because of the great infirmity and sickness of Terah. Terah lived 205 years and died in Haran. Ge 11:31,32

The Third Age of the World

2083 AM, 2793 JP, 1921 BC

71. After Terah died who was Abram's father, God again called Abram from his own country, kindred and his father's house. A further promise and evangelical covenant of blessing was given to him. That is, in his blessed seed, our Lord Jesus Christ, all the nations of the earth would be blessed. Ge 12:1,2 Ac 7:4 **From the time of the giving of this promise and Abram's immediate departure, we mark as the start of those 430 years which Abram and his posterity spent in foreign lands.** Ex 12:40,41 Ga 3:17 The first and last day of this pilgrimage was on the 15th of the month Abib, which in this year was Wednesday, May 4th, according to the Julian Calendar, by our calculations.

72. Therefore, on this day, Abram when he was 75 years old, obeyed the call of God. He took Sarai his wife and Lot, his brother Haran's son, with all the substance, which he had gotten and souls which God had given him in Haran. He took his journey and at length came into the land of Canaan. He passed through it until he came to a place called Sichem, to the oak of Moreh, Ge 12:4-6 which is mentioned later in: Ge 35:4 Jos 24:25,26 Jud 9:6 Here God promised Abram that to his seed he would give that land. He built an altar to the Lord, who had appeared to him there. After leaving there, he went into the hill country, called Luz, later, known by the name of Bethel, toward the east. Ge 28:19 Here he again built an altar and called on the name of the Lord. He continued his journey and came into the south part of that country which borders Egypt. Ge 12:7-9

2084a AM, 2793 JP, 1921 BC
73. A famine caused Abram to leave there and go down into Egypt. To avoid danger, Sarah his wife said she was his sister. She was taken into Pharaoh's (Apophi) house. She returned unharmed, not long after that with many gifts and presents. They were given safe passage and allowed to depart from Egypt. Ge 12:10-20

74. Abram, with Lot returned to Canaan. The country which they chose, was not able to feed both their herds of cattle. Therefore they parted and Lot went into the country of Sodom. After his departure, the promise both of the possession of that land of Canaan and also of his numberless posterity was again renewed to him. He left that place between Bethel and Hai, where he had formerly built an altar and dwelt in the plain of Mamre near Hebron. There he built an altar to the Lord. Ge 13:4

2091 AM, 2801 JP, 1913 BC

75. Bera king of Sodom, with the rest of the petty kings of Pentapolis rebelled and shook off the yoke of Chedorlaomer king of Elam, in the 13th year of their subjection to him. Ge 14:4

2092 AM, 2802 JP, 1912 BC

76. In the 14th year Chedorlaomer, with other confederate princes, Amraphel of Shinar, Arioch of Ellasar and Tidal king of the nations, combined their forces against those petty kings who had revolted from him. They first destroyed the Raphaims, the Zuzims, the Emims and the Horites, who inhabited all that region, which afterward was possessed by the Amalekites and the Ammonites. After that, they routed the kings of Pentapolis in the valley of Siddim and carried away Lot prisoner with all the plunder of Sodom and Gomorrah. When tidings came to Abram, he armed 318 of his own servants. With his confederates Aner, Eshcol and Mamre, they overtook Chedorlaomer and his army at Dan with the prey they had gotten. There they defeated and slew them and pursued them to Hobah, on the left of Damascus. They rescued Lot and the rest of the prisoners from the enemies' hands, and brought them back again with all that they had lost. When Abram returned from the slaughter of Chedorlaomer and the other kings, Melchizedek the king of Salem met him and blessed him. He was a priest of the Most High God. Abram, in return offered him the tithe of the spoil which he had taken. He kept nothing of the spoil for himself, but restored to every man his own possessions again. What was not owned he left to his troops for their service. Ge 14:1-24

77. Abram was grieved because he had no heir. Hence, God promised him a posterity equal to the stars of heaven in number. After 400 years sojourning and affliction in a land that was not theirs, God said he would bring them into the

land promised to Abram and bound his word with a covenant to perform it. Ge 15:1-21

2093 AM, 2803 JP, 1911 BC
78. Sarai was longing for that blessed seed. Since ten years had passed since they came into the land of Canaan, she gave to Abram, Hagar her Egyptian servant, for a wife. Hagar conceived a child by her master Abram. She was badly treated by Sarai for her insolence. She fled from Sarai but being warned of God by his angel, she returned and submitted herself to Sarai. Ge 16:13,14

2094b AM, 2804 JP, 1910 BC
79. When Abram was 86 years old, Hagar bore him Ishmael. Ge 16:15-17 17:24,25

2096d AM, 2806 JP, 1908 BC
80. Arphaxad, the third from Noah, died 403 years after the birth of Salem. Ge 11:13

2107c AM, 2817 JP, 1897 BC
81. God made a covenant with Abram, when he was now 99 years old concerning the seed of Isaac. He was to be born of Sarai about that time twelve months later. God gave him the sign of circumcision (changing both their names, Abram into Abraham and Sarai into Sarah) for a sure pledge and testimony of his promise. He promised also to favour Ishmael the firstborn, for his father's sake. These promises Abraham received and embraced with a true faith. Hence in true obedience, caused himself, being now 99 years of age and his son Ishmael then 13 years old and all his household, to be circumcised, the same day it was commanded him. Ge 17:21-26

82. Abraham invited angels, who looked like travelling men, into his house and gave them a feast. These angels reiterated the promise of the birth of Isaac for Sarah's sake. They

foretold the judgment God intended upon the 5 cities, for their utter destruction. Abraham, fearing what would become of Lot and his family in Sodom, made intercession to God for the sparing of that place. Ge 18:23-33 Therefore Sodom, Gomorrah, Adamah and Zeboiim, for their horrible sins, perished by fire and brimstone that rained down upon them from heaven. Ge 19:1-29 These cities were to be an example to all wicked men in times to come, of the pains of that everlasting fire to be inflicted on them in the lake of fire and brimstone, which is the second death. 2Pe 2:6,7 Re 19:20 20:10 21:8 The monument of this remains to this day, even the Dead Sea. The valley of Siddim, where these five cities stood in former times was full of brimstone and salt pits. This has since grown into a vast lake, which from the brimstone still floating in it, is called "Laces Asphaltitis", a Lake of Brimstone and from the salt, "Mare Salsum", the Salt Sea. /APC Wis 10:6,7 Ge 14:3,10 De 3:17 29:23 Zep 2:9 Of this, Solinus thus writes:

``A great way off from Jerusalem, there lies a woeful spectacle, of a country to be seen, which was blasted from heaven and appears by the blackness of the earth falling all to cinders. There were in that place before this two cities, one called Sodom, the other Gomorrah, where if an apple grew, though it seems to have a show of maturity and ripeness, yet it is not eatable at all. The outer skin of it, contains nothing within it save a stinking smell, mingled with ashes and being never so lightly touched, sends forth a smoke and the rest falls presently into a light dust of powder.''

83. Lot was hurried from Sodom by the angels and avoided its destruction, by fleeing to a little city, called Bela also called Zoar. His wife was turned into a pillar of salt. Lot feared to continue at Zoar and left the plain country. He went into the hills, as he was commanded, taking his two daughters with him. Ge 19:30-38

84. Abraham left the plain of Mamre and went towards the south to dwell in a place which was later called Beersheba. He was entertained by Abimelech, king of the Philistines at Gerar. Sarah, once again went by the name of his sister and she was taken from him. After the king was reproved and punished by God, he restored her untouched to her husband. He presented him with large gifts and presents. By Abraham's prayers Abimelech and all his house were healed of their infirmities. Ge 20:1-18

2108c AM, 2818 JP, **1896 BC**
85. **When Abraham was now 100 and Sarah 90 years of age, the promised son Isaac was born to them.** Ge 17:17,21 Ro 4:19 Not long after this, Moab and Amon were born to Lot, who was both father and grandfather to them. Ge 19:36-38

2113c AM, 2823 JP, 1891 BC
86. After Isaac was weaned, Abraham made a great feast. Sarah saw Ishmael the son of Hagar the Egyptian jesting with, or rather "mocking" (as in Ge 39:14 that word is translated) or even "persecuting" (as the apostle, Ga 4:29 expounds it) her son Isaac. Ishmael who was the older, claimed the right of inheritance in his father's estate. Sarah asked Abraham to cast out Ishmael, "for the son of this handmaid shall not be heir with my son Isaac." Though he took this very grievously at first, yet he did it, for God had said to him, "in Isaac shall thy seed be called". Ge21:8,12 Ro 9:7,8 Heb 11:17,18 Hence, we observe that Isaac is called his only begotten son. It was 430 years from the time Abraham left Haran Ga 3:17 Ex 12:41 until the exodus. Abraham was told his seed would be persecuted for 400 years. Based on Ga 4:29, Ge 15:13 Ac 7:6 we conclude that this persecution started at this time when Isaac was 5 years old when Abraham made this feast, 30 years after Abraham left Haran.

``Among the Hebrews there is a difference of opinions. Some hold that this was done in the 5th year after Isaac's weaning, others in the 12th. We, choosing a shorter time of age, reckon that Ishmael was cast out with his mother, when he was 18 years old.''

87. So Jerome says, writing on the traditions of the Jews on Genesis, that from this declaration of the elect seed and persecution (as the apostle terms it) of Isaac, by Hagar's son, many of them, start the 400 year period which the seed of Abraham was to be a stranger and sojourner and afflicted in a foreign land, as God had foretold him. Ge 15:13 Ac 7:6 For those 400 years were to be completed at the same time as the departure of the children of Israel from Egypt, as appears from Ge 15:14 Ex 12:35,36,41 when compared with each other. Although the ordinary gloss from Augustine, refers to the beginning of the account, to the very birth of Isaac, as if the scripture called the number of 405 by the amount of 400 years meaning that the time was a rounded off number.

2126d AM, 2836 JP, 1878 BC
88. Salah the 4th from Noah, died 403 years after the birth of Heber. Ge 11:15

2131b AM, 2841 JP, 1873 BC
89. Assis reigned in Egypt for 49 years, 2 months. {*Manetho, 1:83}

2133 AM, 2843 JP, 1871 BC
90. By faith Abraham, when he was tried, offered up his son Isaac. He considered within himself, that God was able by his power, to raise him again from the dead, whence also he did receive him, in a manner. Heb 11:17,19

91. Josephus says that at this time Isaac was 25 years old. (Antiq. l. 1. c. 13.) He was at that time in his prime of years. This may be deduced from the fact that he was able to carry so much wood for the burning and consuming of such a

whole burnt offering of himself as Abraham intended to make. Ge 22:6

2145c AM, 2855 JP, 1859 BC
92. Sarah died in Hebron at age 127. Abraham bought the cave for her burial in the field of Machpelah from Ephron the Hittite, for a sum of money. This was the first possession that he had in the land of Canaan. Ge 23:1,2,19,20 As Abraham is known to us as the father of the faithful, Ro 4:11,12 so is Sarah as the mother of the faithful. 1Pe 3:6 She is the only woman whose age at death is mentioned in the scripture.

2148b AM, 2858 JP, 1856 BC
93. Abraham was very careful about getting a wife for his son Isaac. He sent his chief servant, Eliezer of Damascus Ge 15:2 (taking first an oath of him) to find one for him. Eliezer under the guidance of God went into Mesopotamia and there obtained for him Rebecca the daughter of Bethuel, sister to Laban the Syrian. Isaac received her for his wife and brought her into the tent of his mother Sarah. By the solace and contentment which he took in her, he dispelled the sadness and grief which he had after the death of his mother, who died 3 years before. Ge 24:1-67 He was 40 years old when he married Rebecca. Ge 25:20

94. About this time began the reign of the Argivi in Peloponesus, 1080 years before the first olympiad, according to Eusebius in his Chronicle reports, from Castor.

95. The first that there reigned was Inachus, who reigned 50 years. Of him Erasmus, in the proverb, "Inacho Antiquior", refers to. Whom also I refer that of the most learned Varro, in his 17th book of "Human Affairs", (cited by A. Gellius in his first book, "Noctium Attic" c. 16. and of Macrobius: l. 1 Saturnal.) where he said, to the beginning of Romulus are reckoned more than 1100 years. For from the beginning of Inachus' reign, according to the calculations of Castor, there

mentioned, to the Palilia, or solemn festivals of Pales (the country goddess among the Romans) mentioned by Varro, are reckoned 1102 years.

2158d AM, 2868 JP, 1846 BC
96**. Shem the son of Noah died** 500 years after the birth of Arphaxad. Ge 11:11

2167d AM, 2877 JP, 1837 BC
97. When Rebecca had been barren for 19 years after her marriage, Isaac in great devotion made prayer to God on her behalf, and she thereupon conceived twins. Ge 25:21

2168c AM, 2878 JP, **1836 BC**
98. When the twins strove in the womb, Rebecca asked counsel of God. God said that two differing and opposing nations should proceed out of her in that birth, of which the one should be stronger than the other, and that the older should serve the younger. But at the time of her travail, the first that came forth was ruddy all over and like to a shag garment and his name was called **Esau**. Then came forth the other, holding the former by the heel, whereupon he was **called by the name of Jacob. Isaac, their father, at the time of their birth, was 60 years old. Ge 25:22; Ho 12:3**

2179 AM, 2889 JP, 1825 BC
99. Manetho wrote {*Manetho, 1:101} that Tethmosis king of Thebais, or the upper Egypt, besieged the Hyksos or Shepherds, shut up in a place called Auarim (containing 10,000 acres of ground) with an army of 480,000 men. When he found no possibility of taking them, he agreed with them that they should leave Egypt and go freely wherever they wished. They, with all their substance and goods, being in number no less than 440,000, passed through Egypt and went by the way of the wilderness into Syria. For fear they had of the Assyrians, who then possessed all Asia, they built themselves a city in the land of Judah, as it is now called. This

city was big enough to hold so large a number of inhabitants, and called it Hierosolyma, i.e. Jerusalem. Manetho states this in Josephus l. 1. contra Appionem Grammaticum, which (Appion in his 4th book of "Egyptian Affaires") calls this king, Amosis. He proves out of the Annals of Ptolemy Mendesius an Egyptian priest, that he was contemporary to Inachus mentioned previously, king of the Argivi, as Tatian the Assyrian (in his Oration against the Greeks) Justin Martyr, (in his Paranetion or Exhortatory to the Greeks) Clemens Alexandrinus in his first book of his Stromata and others do report. All which following Josephus and Justus Tiberiensis understand is meant of the Israelites, because they traded much in sheep, Ge 46:33,34 47:3. Because they went from Egypt into Canaan and therefore imagine that Moses was contemporary with Inachus and was the man that conducted them in that journey. Whereas those things seem rather to refer to the Phoenicians, whom Herodotus (l. 7. c. 89) reports to have come from the Red Sea and settled themselves in Palestine. The departure of the Israelites from Egypt happened many years after Inachus, as the course of this chronology undoubtedly shows.

2180c AM, 2890 JP, 1824 BC
100. When Tethmosis or Amosis drove out these shepherds, he reigned in the lower Egypt for 25 years, 4 months.{*Manetho, 1:101}

2183c AM, 2893 JP, **1821 BC**
101. **Abraham died when he was 175 years old** and 100 years after entering Canaan. He was buried by his two sons, Isaac and Ishmael, in his cave at Machpelah, with Sarah his wife. Ge25:7,10 He lived 15 years after the birth of Jacob, with whom he is said also to have lived in tents. Heb 11:9

2187d AM, 2897 JP, 1817 BC
102. Heber, the 5th from Noah, died 430 years after the birth of his son Peleg. Ge 11:17 This man lived the longest of any who were born after the flood. He out lived Abraham and from him Abraham came first to be surnamed, the Hebrew. Ge 14:13 In later times, all the posterity of his grandchild Jacob, were known by the same name. Ge 40:15 Canaan was called the land of the Hebrews, while the Canaanites were still living there.

2200 AM, 2910 JP, 1804 BC
103. About this time, the promises previously made to Abraham, so it seemed, were fulfilled in his son Isaac. To wit:
1) I will multiply thy seed, as the stars of heaven.
2) To thy seed will I give this land.
3) In thy seed, shall all the nations of the earth be blessed. Ge 26:4

2205d AM, 2915 JP, 1799 BC
104. Chebron reigned in Egypt 13 years. {*Manetho, 1:101}

2208c AM, 2918 JP, 1796 BC
105. When Esau was 40 years old, he took two wives from the land of the Hittites. One was Judith the daughter of Beeri and the other was Bashemath the daughter of Elon. These two wives were very troublesome and a grief to Rebecca. Ge 26:34,35 cf. Ge 27:46 28:8

106. At this time the Ogygian Deluge occurred in the country of Attica 1020 years before the first olympiad. This is reported by Hellanicus, Castor, Thalus, Diodorus Siculus and Alexander Polyhistor in his third book of his Chronography, by Julius Africanus, as we find it in Eusebius' book, de Prap. Evang. Varro says this flood happened 300 years earlier.

2218d AM, 2928 JP, 1786 BC
107. Amenophis reigned in Egypt 20 years, 7 months. {*Manetho, 1:101}

2231b AM, 2941 JP, 1773 BC
108. Abraham's son, Ishmael, died at the age of 137 years. Ge 25:17

2239b AM, 2949 JP, 1765 BC
109. Amessis the sister of Amenophis, reigned in Egypt 21 years, 9 months. {*Manetho, 1:101}

2242 AM, 2952 JP, 1762 BC
110. Euechous began to reign in Chaldea, 224 years before the Arabians. (Julian Africanus) He seems to be the same with Belus of Babylon, or Jupiter Belus, who was worshipped later by the Chaldeans as a god. Isa 46:1 Jer 50:2 51:41

2245a AM, 2954 JP, 1760 BC
111. 44 years before his death, Isaac had grown old and blind. He sent his oldest son Esau to hunt some venison for him. Isaac purposed to bless him when he returned. However, Jacob his younger son, by the subtle counsel of his mother, came disguised in Esau's clothing bringing Isaac's favourite meat. Thus he stole away the blessing, unknown to his father. The blessing, though forgotten, God confirmed ever after to Jacob. By so doing, Jacob incurred his brother's hatred. Jacob journeyed to Mesopotamia to his uncle Laban, to avoid his brother's plan to kill him Ge 27:41 and to find a wife of his own kindred. Ge 28:1 Before he left, he asked for his father's blessing on the trip.

112. On his journey, he saw a vision of a ladder. In this vision, God confirmed to him, all the blessings formerly given to his father. God assured him of his grace and favour for the future. In remembrance of this experience, Jacob set up a pillar. He changed the name of the place from Luz to Bethel and made a vow to God there. When he came to Haran, he

stayed with Laban for a month. He fell in love with Rachel his daughter and agreed to serve Laban 7 years for her. Ge 27:1 29:20 Ho 12:12 Jacob was 77 years old in 2259 AM.

113. When Esau knew Isaac had blessed Jacob and sent him away into Mesopotamia to find a wife there and that Jacob did not like the daughters of Canaan, he tried to pacify his father's mind. Isaac was offended with him for marrying his first wife from Canaan. Therefore he took a second wife Mahalath, the daughter of Ishmael, the son of Abraham, Ge 28:6,9

114. Esau had been now a married man 37 years and was 77 years old. Jacob, who was as old as he, had all this while lived a bachelor. Remembering his father's command, he asked Rachel his wife to be given to him because he had served the allotted time for her. Ge 29:21 He was now of an age suitable for marriage, as Tremellius explains it. Tho. Lidyate understands this to have happened after the first month he was with Laban. However Laban intended from the beginning to make full use of Jacob's industry and his managerial skills before he would give his daughter to Jacob. This no doubt, was mentioned when Jacob first arrived since this was the main purpose for his coming.

115. However, by Laban's fraud, instead of Rachel, Leah, the older daughter, was put into Jacob's bed on the marriage night. Nevertheless, at the end of the marriage week, Jud 14:12,17 Rachel also was espoused to him on the condition that Jacob of would serve seven more years for her. Laban gave to Leah, his maid servant Zilpah for a handmaid and to Rachel he gave Bilhah.

116. When Leah was not so favoured by Jacob as Rachel was, God made Rachel barren and Leah was made a mother of 4 children in 4 successive years. Ge 29:21-30:24

2246 AM, 2956 JP, 1758 BC

117. Leah bore Reuban, Jacob's firstborn. Ge 29:32 For his incest committed with Bilhah, his father's concubine, Reuben later lost his birthright. Ge 35:22 49:3,4 1Ch 5:1

2247 AM, 2957 JP, 1757 BC

118. Simeon was born.

2248 AM, 2958 JP, 1756 BC

119. Levi was born Ge 34:34
 (Ddd note: Pdf Scripture in error. Should be Ge 29:34)

2249c AM, 2959 JP, **1755 BC**

120. **Judah was born Ge 35:35** from whom the Jews took their name.
(Ddd note: Pdf Scripture error. Should be Ge 29:35. Per Ussher, Jacob was born 1836BC. This would make Jacob 81 years old when Judah was born)

2259c AM, 2969 JP, **1745 BC**

121. **God blessed Rachel and she bore Joseph** to Jacob at the end of his 14 years of service. Jacob asked permission from Laban to return into his own country. He remained there 6 more years on another condition made between him and his father-in-law Laban for a certain part of his flock. Ge 30:22,25,31 31:41 **Now Jacob was 91 years old when Joseph was born** and consequently, 77 years old, when he first began to serve Laban. This can be deduced for Jacob was 130 years old, when he first stood before Pharaoh, at the time when the 7 years of plenty were passed and 2 years of the famine were over. Ge 45:6 47:9 Joseph was then 39 years old. He was 30 years old when he first came before Pharaoh, just before the 7 years of plenty. Ge 41:32,46

2261a AM, 2970 JP, 1744 BC

122. Mephres reigned in Egypt, 12 years, 9 months. {*Manetho, 1:101}

2265c AM, 2975 JP, 1739 BC

123. As the jealousy and malice grew between Laban and his sons against Jacob, God warned him to return to his own country. Jacob told his wives of this. When Laban was shearing his sheep, at the latter end of the spring (See note on 2974c AM <<439>>) after 20 years of service, Jacob secretly fled from Laban. He took all his goods, wives and family and crossed over the river Euphrates. Ge 31:1,3,19,21,38,41 It is said Jacob had 12 sons born to him in Mesopotamia. Ge 35:22,26 Benjamin is not to be counted among them because he was born later in the land of Canaan near Bethlehem. Ge 16:18,19 In like manner, as the 12 apostles are counted to make up that number even though Judas was dead. Joh 20:24 1Co 15:1 Concerning this matter, see Augustine in his 117th question upon Genesis.

124. Three days later, Laban (for he was three days journey from the place where Jacob kept his sheep) heard that his son-in-law was gone and took some of his friends and kindred with him. After travelling seven days he caught up with him at Mount Gilead. This mount was named from this meeting. After many arguments, they finally reconciled. For a testimony and monument to their covenant and agreement, Jacob erected a pillar, with a heap of stones. Laban the Syrian, called it "Jegar Sahadutha", but Jacob the Hebrew called it "Galeed", i.e. "the heap of a testimony", or "witness" between the two. Ge 31:47,48

125. After Jacob left Laban in peace, he was frightened by the news of his brother Esau's coming with a band of men. He divided his company into two groups and called on God. He sent ahead of him presents to his brother Esau. After wrestling with the angel, he was given the name of Israel by God. Jacob matured spiritually by depending more on the help of God than on man. Ge 32:1-32 Ho 12:3,4

126. Esau entertained his brother courteously. After much entreaty he accepted Jacob's presents and offered to escort him on his way. When Jacob refused, Esau left. Then Jacob went on to Succoth. He called the place Succoth because he built an house there and cotes for his sheep. After passing over Jordan, he came into Canaan and pitched his tent in Shechem, a city of the Shechemites. He bought a parcel of ground from the sons of Hamor the Shechemite, for 100 pieces of silver. There he built an altar, which he called by the name of "El-Elohe-Israel" or "The mighty God, the God of Israel." Ge 33:1-20 It was in this same place that Abraham had built his first altar before: Ge 12:6,7 and where Jacob's well was, near to Mount Gerizim. When the woman of Samaria spoke to our Saviour, she said that her fathers worshipped in this mountain. Joh 4:5,6,12,20 This mountain was located in the country of the Shechemites. Jud 9:7

2273d AM, 2983 JP, 1731 BC
127. Mephramuthosis reigned in Egypt 25 years, 10 months. {*Manetho, 1:101}

2276c AM, 2986 JP, 1728 BC
128. When Joseph was 17 years old, he told his father of his brothers' wickedness and was told by God that he would one day be the head of all his father's family. His brothers hated him for this so much that they plotted his death. At length they agreed to sell him for a slave into a far country. When they drew him from the pit that they had cast him into, they sold him for 20 pieces of silver to the Ishmaelite and Midianite merchants. Both of these peoples descended from their grandfather Abraham. Joseph was carried away by them to Egypt. There they sold him to be a slave to Potiphar, the captain of Pharaoh's guard. Ge 37:2,3,6 Justin also, in his Epitome of Troeus Pompeius, l. 36. c. 2. makes mention of Joseph. He says: ``His brothers envied the excellency of his wisdom. After getting him privately into their hands, they sold him to foreign merchants who carried him into Egypt.''

2287c AM, 2997 JP, 1717 BC
129. When Joseph, was thrown into prison, he interpreted the dreams of two officers of Pharaoh's court. This was two years before he was brought before Pharaoh. Ge 40:1-41:1

2288c AM, 2998 JP, 1716 BC
130. Isaac died at the age of 180 years and was buried by his two sons, Esau and Jacob. Ge 35:28,29

2289b AM, 2999 JP, 1715 BC
131. When Pharaoh could not get his dreams interpreted by his own wise men, and after hearing of Joseph's skill in expounding dreams, he sent for Joseph. He was 30 years old when he explained the king's dreams. The first dream was that of the 7 years of plenty followed by 7 years famine. Moreover, he advised Pharaoh how to provide from the abundance of the first 7 years of plenty, for the famine of the next 7 years of scarcity. Thereupon Pharaoh, by the general agreement of all his nobles, made him governor of the whole kingdom. He gave him a wife, Asenath, the daughter of Potiphar, governor of On or Heliopolis in Egypt. Ge 41:1-46 Justin also from Trogus Pompeius says, that he was very important to Pharaoh. For he said:
``Joseph was most skilled in explaining dreams or signs and was the first that found out and taught the art of the interpretation of dreams. Neither was there any part of divine or human intention, which seemed to be unknown to him in that he foretold a famine many years before it happened. All Egypt would have perished unless the king, by his advice, had ordered grain to be stored many years before the famine came.''

132. From the harvest of this year started the 7 years of plenty. In these years Joseph laid up an enormous supply of grain. Asenath, his wife, bore him two sons, Manasseh and Ephraim. Ge 41:47,51,53

2296c AM, 3006 JP, 1708 BC
133. The 7 years of the famine began from the harvest of this year as predicted. Joseph's wisdom in laying up supplies not only sustained Egypt but also helped relieve the famine in the neighbouring countries. Ge 41:54,57

2297d AM, 3007 JP, 1707 BC
134. Jacob sent 10 of his sons into Egypt to buy grain. Joseph pretended not to know them and took them for spies. They were held and not released until Simeon, the oldest and the leader of them, who consented to sell Joseph, was cast into prison. He was held to ensure that the rest should bring to Joseph, Benjamin, their youngest brother, who was born of Rachel, Joseph's own mother. When they were sent away, they carried their grain and the money they had payed for it. This money was placed into each of their sacks by the secret orders of Joseph. They told their father Jacob, all that had happened to them. Also they told him it was necessary that their youngest brother Benjamin return with them to Egypt. They were not able to convince Jacob to allow this to happen. Ge 42:1-38

2298b AM, 3008 JP, 1706 BC
135. When Jacob was hard pressed by the famine, he sent his sons again and with them Benjamin their brother. He sent twice the amount of money needed to buy grain and other gifts for Joseph. When they arrived, they were courteously entertained and feasted by Joseph. Simeon was released and returned to them. Ge 43:1-34

136. When they were on their way home, Joseph arrested them for stealing his cup. This he had caused secretly to be hidden in Benjamin's sack. When they were confronted with this crime, they tried to show their honesty by the fact that they returned the money they found in their sacks when they came into Egypt the second time. They offered to die, or to

be his slaves, if any such thing could be proved against them. But in the end the cup was found with Benjamin. They returned to Joseph and yielded themselves to him to be his slaves. When Joseph refused and said he would have no one but him with whom the cup was found, Judah then humbly offered himself to serve him in Benjamin's stead. Ge 44:1-34

137. When Joseph heard Judah make this offer, he revealed himself to his brothers. The brothers were all terrified at the remembrance of the sin which they had committed against Joseph. He comforted them by showing how that deed of theirs was an act of God's providence. From the king's supplies, Joseph ordered wagons and provisions for their journey. They were to go and to return with all speed, bringing their father and their families with them. When they told their father, he did not believe them, until he saw the wagons and other supplies necessary for them to move to Egypt. Ge 45:1-28

138. After Jacob offered sacrifices and was encouraged by God, he and all his family, went down into Egypt. This was in the beginning of the third year of the famine when Jacob was 130 years old. Ge 45:6 46:1,27 47:9 De 26:5

139. After Joseph had told Pharaoh of the arrival of his family in Egypt, he brought his father and 5 of his brothers to Pharaoh. When Pharaoh had communed with them, he assigned them a suitable place in the land of Goshen where Joseph took care of all their needs. Ge 47:1-12

2299d AM, 3009 JP, 1705 BC
140. Mephramuthosis died and Thmosis reigned in Egypt for 9 years 8 months. {*Manetho, 1:101}

2300 AM, 3010 JP, 1704 BC
141. Joseph took all the money in Egypt and Canaan from the grain that he had sold to them. Ge47:14

2301 AM, 3011 JP, 1703 BC
142. When all the money of both these countries was spent, the Egyptians sold all their flocks and herds of cattle to Joseph for food to live on that year. Ge 47:15-17

2302 AM, 3012 JP, 1702 BC
143. At the end of this year, when their money and stock of cattle was all gone, the Egyptians then sold both their lands and freedom to Joseph. He supplied them with grain for food and with seed to plant in this seventh and last year of the famine. He was to be repaid in the year following, when the famine was over. So that Pharaoh would have a clear title and full possession of the lands he purchased, Joseph moved everyone from one side of the country to the other.
There he assigned to every man land to till and to work. From the profits a law was made giving Pharaoh a fifth part of the increase. Only the chief governors' and the priests' lands, were not bought by Pharaoh. These individuals had a living by the king's allowance and had no need to sell their lands for food as others had.

2309b AM, 3019 JP, 1695 BC
144. Amenophis reigned in Egypt 30 years 10 months. {*Manetho, 1:103}

2315 AM, 3025 JP, **1689 BC**
145. When **Jacob** was about to die, he adopted Ephraim and Manasseh the sons of Joseph. He blessed them by revelation from God and set the younger ahead of the older. Ge 48:1-22 Heb 11:12 When he called his sons together, he blessed them all and foretold what should befall them in the coming generations. He told them that memorable prophesy of the

Messiah and gave orders to them concerning his burial. He **died at 147 years of age** 17 years of which were in the land of Egypt. Ge 49:1-33 47:25

...

2369c AM, 3079 JP, 1635 BC

148. By faith, Joseph on his death bed spoke of the departure of the children of Israel from Egypt. He asked that his bones might be carried with them. He was 110 years old when he died and saw his children to the third generation. Ge 50:22-26 Heb 11:22 These were Shuthelah and Tahan, the grandsons of Ephraim and Eran or Taran, Nu 26:36 the sons of Manasseh and Gilead was Manasseh's grandchild. From here it is, that the Greek expositors, speaking of the families of Jacob and Joseph, which were said to consist of 70 souls, Ge 46:27 De 10:22 adding to the total these 5 who were born to Joseph in Egypt 1Ch 7:20-29 for a number of 75 persons in all. **It appears that Joseph ruled and governed the state of Egypt for 80 years under several Pharaohs.** Eusebius in his chronicle, has rightly observed and summarised it thus: ``Joseph was made governor of Egypt when he was 30 years old and when his father Jacob was 122 years old. He headed the government for 80 years. After he died, **the Hebrews were held in bondage by the Egyptians 144 years. Therefore, the whole time which the Hebrews spent in Egypt was 215 years**, starting from the time that Jacob and his sons went down into Egypt."

149. The book of Genesis ends with the death of Joseph and contains the history of 2369 years. This book was written by Moses. This is the opinion of the Talmudists in their Bababathra l. 1. and so it is generally believed by all the Hebrews. The sum of it is delivered by "Servins Sulpicins", in the first book of his "Historia Sacras"...

...

2430b AM, 3140 JP, **1574 BC**

160. **Aaron was born 3 years before his brother Moses,** 83 years before the departure of the Israelites from Egypt. Ex 7:7

...

2433 AM, 3143 JP, **1571 BC**

162. 41 years after the death of her father Levi, **Jochebed bore Moses to Amram,** her nephew and husband. Moses was 80 years old, when he first spoke to Pharaoh to let the children of Israel go. Ex 7:7 40 years later Moses died in the 12th month when he was 120 years old. De 3:1,2 34:7

...

2513b AM, 3223 JP, **1491 BC**

...

190. On the 15th day of the 1st month (Tuesday, May 5th) at midnight, the firstborn of all Egypt were slain. **Pharaoh and his servants, quickly sent away the Israelites** with all their goods and the plunder which they had received from the Egyptians. Ex 12:33,35,36 **It was exactly 430 years from the first pilgrimage of Abraham's departure from Canaan,** to the day they were set free from bondage.

...

2514c AM, 3224 JP, **1490 BC**

...

224. On this first day, **Naasson,** (from whom David and according to the flesh, Jesus Christ himself) came and made his offering for the tribes of Judah. Then the rest, every one for his tribe, according to the order as they were ranked in their camps, made offerings. Nu 7:11-83

...

2553b AM, 3263 JP, **1451 BC**

...

297. In the 12th month of this year, **Moses** left the plain of Moab and climbed up Mount Nebo which was a part of the country of Abarim. From the top of it facing Jericho, he beheld all the land of promise and then **died at the age of 120 years**. Nu 27:12,13 De 3:23-29, 32:49,50 34:1-5, 31:2-4,7 Of this time he spent 40 years less a month in governing the people of Israel. This is confirmed by Josephus, in the end of his 4th book of antiquities. He states that Moses died on the first day of the last month of the year.

...

2553c AM, 3263 JP, **1451 BC**

...

311. Our Lord Jesus, the Captain of his Father's Host, appeared to Joshua, (the type of Jesus), before Jericho with a drawn sword in his hand. Jesus there promised to defend his people. Jos 5:13-15

312. The Ark of God was carried around Jericho for seven days. On the 7th day, the walls of Jericho fell down flat when the priests blew their trumpets. The city was taken and utterly destroyed. All were killed except for Rahab and her family. Jos 6:1-27 **Later** she married **Salmon** of the tribe of Judah and they had a son called **Boaz.** Mt 1:5

...

2919c AM, 3629 JP, **1085 BC**

394. **David** was born to Jesse the Ephrathite in his old age.**1Sa 17:12** David was the youngest of eight sons born to Jesse. Bethlehem was called the City of David 1Sa 20:6 Lu 2:4 30 years before he succeeded Saul in the kingdom. 2Sa 5:4 1Sa 16:1

*Ddd note:1 Sam 17:12 the scripture does **not** clearly state that Jesse was old when he had David, but only that Jesse earned a reputation of being old at the time of Saul.*

"Now David was the son of that Ephrathite of Beth-lehem-judah, whose name was Jesse; and he had eight sons: and the man went among men for an old man in the days of Saul."

...

2971a AM, 3680 JP, **1034 BC**

(DDD note: David would be 51 years old)

435. Bathsheba who was now David's wife, bore David another son whose name was given to him by God **called Solomon.** This child proved to be a man of peace.1Ch 22:9 His name means one beloved of God, the name of Jedidiah. 2Sa 12:25

...

The Fifth Age of the World

2992c AM, 3702 JP, **1012 BC**
465. **The foundation of the temple was laid** in the 480th year after Israel's exodus from Egypt. This was in king Solomon's 4th year of reign on the second day of the second month (called Zif, Monday May 21st). 1Ki 6:1,37 2Ch 3:2

3012c AM, 3722 JP, **992 BC**
471. In the 13th year after **the temple was built**, Solomon finished building his own house. He spent 20 years on both of them: 7 years 5 months on the temple and 13 years on his own house. 1Ki 7:1 9:10 2Ch 8:1

The Seventh Age of the World

4000a AM, 4709 JP, **5 BC**
...
6057. **Jesus Christ and Son of God, in the fulness of time was born** of the most blessed virgin Mary, at Bethlehem. {Mt 1:25 2:1,5 Ga 4:4} Mary wrapped him in swaddling clothes and laid him in a manger because there was no room in the inn. {Lu 2:7}
...
4000b AM, 4710 JP, **4 BC**
6060. **The wise men from the east were guided by a star and came to Herod at Jerusalem**. They were told that the birth place of **Christ** was in Bethlehem of Judea. They went there and entering into the house which was showed to them by the star that stood over it. They found the little child with Mary, his mother. They fell down and worshipped him and gave their treasures to him, gold, frankincense and myrrh. They were warned by God in a dream that they should not return to Herod and so they departed into their own country by another way. {Mt 2:1-12}

10. The Inspired Version

The following are excerpts from the Inspired Version (also known as the Joseph Smith Translation), particularly relevant to the subject of this book and provides a primary source for the Doddridge Chronology.

Ddd Notes are added occasionally to clarify a statement., as *Ddd Note: ....*

Inspired Version*

The Holy Scriptures
CONTAINING THE OLD AND NEW TESTAMENTS
AN INSPIRED REVISION OF THE
AUTHORIZED VERSION
BY JOSEPH SMITH, JUNIOR

** Source: see Bibliography, Smith Jr., Joseph*

GENESIS, CHAPTER 6

Adam warns men to repent – Seth is born -- The priesthood is shown - Book of generations kept – Satan has dominion -- God's promise to Enoch -- Enoch's vision – His preaching.

1 And Adam hearkened unto the voice of God, and called upon his sons to repent.

2 And Adam knew his wife again, and she bare a son, and he called his name Seth.

3 And Adam glorified the name of God, for he said, God hath appointed me another seed instead of Abel whom Cain slew.

4 And God revealed himself unto Seth, and he rebelled not, but offered an acceptable sacrifice like unto his brother Abel. And to him also was born a son, and he called his name Enos.

5 And then began these men to call upon the name of the Lord; and the Lord blessed them; and a book of remembrance was kept in the which was recorded in the

language of Adam, for it was given unto as many as called upon God, to write by the Spirit of inspiration;

6 And by them their children were taught to read and write, having a language which was pure and undefiled.

7 Now this same priesthood which was in the beginning, shall be in the end of the world also.

8 Now this prophecy Adam spake, as he was moved upon by the Holy Ghost.

9 And a genealogy was kept of the children of God. And this was the book of the generations of Adam, saying, In the day that God created man, (in the likeness of God made he him), in the image of his own body, male and female created he them, and blessed them, and called their name Adam, in the day when they were created, and became living souls, in the land, upon the footstool of God.

10 And **Adam lived one hundred and thirty years, and begat a son** in his own likeness, after his own image, and called his name **Seth.**

11 And the days of Adam, after he had begotten Seth, were eight hundred years. And he begat many sons and daughters. And all the days that **Adam lived, were nine hundred and thirty years; and he died.**

12 **Seth lived one hundred and five years, and begat Enos**, and prophesied in all his days, and taught his son Enos in the ways of God. Wherefore Enos prophesied also. And Seth lived after he begat Enos, eight hundred and seven years, and begat many sons and daughters.

(Ddd note: 105 + 807 = 912)

13 And the children of men were numerous upon all the face of the land. And in those days, Satan had great dominion among men, and raged in their hearts; and from thenceforth came wars and bloodshed.

14 And a man's hand was against his own brother in administering death, because of secret works, seeking for power. And all the days of Seth were nine hundred and twelve years; and he died.

15 And **Enos lived ninety years, and begat Cainan**. And Enos, and the residue of the people of God, came out from the land which was called Shulon, and dwelt in a land of promise, which he called after his own son, whom he had named Cainan.

16 And Enos lived, after he begat Cainan, eight hundred and fifteen years, and begat many sons and daughters. **And all the days of Enos were nine hundred and five years; and he died.**

17 And **Cainan lived seventy years, and begat Mahalaleel.**

18 And Cainan lived after he begat Mahalaleel, eight hundred and forty years, and begat sons and daughters. **And all the days of Cainan were nine hundred and ten years; and he died.**

19 And **Mahalaleel lived sixty-five years, and begat Jared.**

20 And Mahalaleel lived after he begat Jared, eight hundred and thirty years, and begat sons and daughters. **And all the days of Mahalaleel were eight hundred and ninety-five years; and he died.**

21 And **Jared lived one hundred and sixty-two years, and begat Enoch.**

22 And Jared lived, after he begat Enoch, eight hundred years, and begat sons and daughters. And Jared taught Enoch in all the ways of God.

(Ddd note: 162 + 800 = 962)

23 And this is the genealogy of the sons of Adam, who was the son of God, with whom God himself conversed.

24 And they were preachers of righteousness, and spake and prophesied, and called upon all men everywhere to repent. And faith was taught unto the children of men.

25 And it came to pass, that all the days of Jared were nine hundred and sixty-two years; and he died.

26 And **Enoch lived sixty-five years, and begat Methuselah.** And it came to pass that Enoch journeyed in the land, among the people; and as he journeyed the Spirit of God descended out of heaven, and abode upon him;

27 And he heard a voice from heaven, saying, Enoch, my son, prophesy unto this people, and say unto them, Repent, for thus saith the Lord, I am angry with this people, and my fierce anger is kindled against them; for their hearts have waxed hard, and their ears are dull of hearing, and their eyes cannot see afar off.

...

GENESIS, CHAPTER 7

...

75 And the Lord showed Enoch all things, even unto the end of the world. And he saw the day of the righteous, the hour of their redemption, and received a fullness of joy.

76 And all the days of Zion, in the days of Enoch, were three hundred and sixty-five years.

77 And Enoch and all his people walked with God, and he dwelt in the midst of Zion.

78 And it came to pass, that Zion was not, for God received it up into his own bosom; and from thence went forth the saying, Zion is fled. **And all the days of Enoch were four hundred and thirty years.**

79 And it came to pass, that Methuselah, the son of Enoch, was not taken, that the covenants of the Lord might be fulfilled which he made to Enoch; for he truly covenanted with Enoch, that Noah should be of the fruit of his loins.

80 And it came to pass, that Methuselah prophesied that from his loins should spring all the kingdoms of the earth; (through Noah), and he took glory unto himself.

81 And there came forth a great famine into the land, and the Lord cursed the earth with a sore curse, and many of the inhabitants thereof died.

82 And it came to pass, that **Methuselah lived one hundred and eighty seven years, and begat Lamech;** and Methuselah lived after he begat Lamech, seven hundred and eighty two years, and begat sons and daughters. **And all the days of Methuselah were nine hundred and sixty-nine years, and he died.**

83 And Lamech lived one hundred and eighty-two years, and begat a son, and he called his name Noah, saying, This son shall comfort us concerning our work, and toil of our hands, because of the ground which the Lord hath cursed.

84 And Lamech lived after he begat Noah, five hundred and ninety-five years, and begat sons and daughters. **And all the days of Lamech were seven hundred and seventy-seven years; and he died.**

85 And **Noah was four hundred and fifty years old,** and begat Japheth, and **forty-two years afterwards, he begat Shem**, of her who was the mother of Japheth, and when he was five hundred years old, he begat Ham.

GENESIS, CHAPTER 8

God displeased because Noah's daughters sell themselves – Noah declares the gospel -- The earth filled with violence -- The flood foretold -- The ark made -- Commandment of Noah -- Two by two, the male and his female saved -- The ark rests, the waters abate.

1 And Noah and his sons hearkened unto the Lord, and gave heed; and they were called the sons of God.

2 And when these men began to multiply on the face of the earth, and daughters were born unto them, the sons of men saw that their daughters were fair, and they took them wives even as they chose.

3 And the Lord said unto Noah, The daughters of thy sons have sold themselves, for behold, mine anger is kindled against the sons of men, for they will not hearken to my voice.

4 And it came to pass, that Noah prophesied, and taught the things of God, even as it was in the beginning.

5 And the Lord said unto Noah, My Spirit shall not always strive with man, for he shall know that all flesh shall die, yet his days shall be an hundred and twenty years; and if men do not repent, I will send in the floods upon them.

6 And in those days there were giants on the earth, and they sought Noah to take away his life;

7 But the Lord was with Noah, and the power of the Lord was upon him; and the Lord ordained Noah after his own order, and commanded him that he should go forth and declare his gospel unto the children of men, even as it was given unto Enoch.

8 And it came to pass that Noah called upon the children of men, that they should repent, but they hearkened not unto his words.

9 And also, after that they had heard him, they came up before him, saying, Behold, we are the sons of God, have we not taken unto ourselves the daughters of men? and are we not eating and drinking, and marrying and given in marriage? and our wives bear unto us children, and the same are mighty men, which are like unto them of old, men of great renown. And they hearkened not unto the words of Noah.

10 And God saw that the wickedness of man had become great in the earth; and every man was lifted up in the imagination of the thoughts of his heart; being only evil continually.

11 And it came to pass, that Noah continued his preaching unto the people, saying, Hearken and give heed unto my words, believe and repent of your sins and be baptized in the name of Jesus Christ, the Son of God, even as our fathers did, and ye shall receive the Holy Ghost, that ye may have all things made manifest;

12 And if you do not this, the floods will come in upon you; nevertheless, they hearkened not.

13 And it repented Noah, and his heart was pained, that the Lord had made man on the earth, and it grieved him at his heart.

14 And the Lord said, I will destroy man **whom I have created**, from the face of the earth, both man and beast, and the creeping things, and the fowls of the air.

15 For it repenteth Noah that I have created them, and that I have made them; and he hath called upon me, for they have sought his life.

16 And thus Noah found grace in the eyes of the Lord; for Noah was a just man, and perfect in his generation; and he walked with God, and also his three sons, Shem, Ham, and Japheth.

17 The earth was corrupt before God; and it was filled with violence. And God looked upon the earth, and behold, it was corrupt, for all flesh had corrupted its way upon the earth.

18 And God said unto Noah, The end of all flesh is come before me; for the earth is filled with violence, and behold, I will destroy all flesh from off the earth.

19 Make thee therefore, an ark of gopher wood; rooms shalt thou make in the ark, and thou shalt pitch it within and without with pitch;

20 And the length of the ark thou shalt make three hundred cubits; the breadth of it fifty cubits; and the height of it thirty cubits.

21 And windows shalt thou make to the ark, and in a cubit shalt thou finish it above; and the door of the ark shalt thou set in the side thereof; lower, second, and third chambers shalt thou make in it.

22 And behold, I, even I will bring in a flood of water upon the earth, to destroy all flesh, wherein is the breath of life, from under heaven; every thing that liveth on the earth shall die.

23 But with thee will I establish my covenant, even as I have sworn unto thy father, Enoch, that of thy posterity shall come all nations.

24 And thou shalt come into the ark, thou and thy sons, and thy wife, and thy sons' wives with them.

25 And of every living thing of all flesh, two of every kind shalt thou bring into the ark, to keep alive with thee; they shall be male and female.

26 Of fowls after their kind, and of cattle after their kind, of every creeping thing of the earth after his kind; two of every kind shalt thou take into the ark, to keep alive.

27 And take thou unto thee of all food that is eaten, and thou shalt gather fruit of every kind unto thee in the ark, and it shall be for food for thee, and for them.

28 Thus did Noah, according to all that God commanded him.

29 And the Lord said unto Noah, Come thou and all thy house, into the ark; for thee only have I seen righteous before me, in this generation.

30 Of every clean beast thou shalt take to thee by sevens, the male and his female; and of beasts that are not clean by two, the male and his female;

31 Of fowls also of the air, by sevens, the male and his female; to keep seed alive upon the face of the earth.

32 For yet seven days, and I will cause it to rain upon the earth forty days, and forty nights; and every living substance that I have made will I destroy from off the face of the earth.

33 And Noah did according to all that the Lord commanded him. And Noah was six hundred years old when the flood of waters was upon the earth.

34 And Noah went in, and his sons, and his wife, and his sons' wives with him, into the ark, because of the waters of the flood.

35 Of clean beasts, and of beasts that were not clean, and of fowls, and of every thing that creepeth upon the earth, there went in two and two, unto Noah into the ark, the male and the female, as God had commanded Noah.

36 And it came to pass, after seven days, that the waters of the flood were upon the earth. **In the six hundredth year of Noah's life,** in the second month, and the seventeenth day of the month, the same day were all the fountains of the great deep broken up, and the windows of heaven were opened, and the rain was upon the earth forty days and forty nights.

37 In the selfsame day entered Noah, and Shem, and Ham, and Japheth, the sons of Noah; and Noah's wife, and the three wives of his sons with them into the ark; they, and every beast after his kind, and all the cattle after their kind, and every creeping thing that creepeth on the earth, after his kind, and every fowl after his kind, and every bird of every sort;

38 And they went unto Noah, into the ark, two and two of all flesh, wherein is the breath of life; and they that went in, went in male and female of all flesh, as God had commanded him, and the Lord shut him in.

39 And the flood was forty days upon the earth, and the waters increased, and bare up the ark, and it was lifted up above the earth.

40 And the waters prevailed and increased greatly upon the earth, and the ark went upon the face of the waters.

41 And the waters prevailed exceedingly upon the face of the earth, and all the high hills, under the whole heavens were covered. Fifteen cubits and upward did the waters prevail; and the mountains were covered.

42 And all flesh died that moved upon the face of the earth, both of fowl, and of cattle, and of beasts, and of every creeping thing that creepeth upon the earth, and every man.

43 All in whose nostrils the Lord had breathed the breath of life, of all that were on the dry land, died.

44 And every living substance was destroyed, which was upon the face of the ground, both man, and cattle, and the creeping things, and the fowls of the air; and they were destroyed from the earth;

45 And Noah only remained, and they that were with him in the ark.

46 And the waters prevailed on the earth one hundred and fifty days.

47 And God remembered Noah, and all that were with him in the ark. And God made a wind to pass over the earth, and the waters assuaged.

48 The fountains also of the deep, and the windows of heaven were stopped, and the rain from heaven was restrained; and the waters returned from off the earth.

49 And after the end of the hundred and fifty days, the waters were abated. And the ark rested in the seventh month, on the seventeenth day of the month, upon the mountain of Ararat.

50 And the waters decreased until the tenth month; and in the tenth month, on the first day of the month, were the tops of the mountains seen.

51 And it came to pass, at the end of forty days, that Noah opened the window of the ark which he had made, and he sent

forth a raven, which went forth to and fro, until the waters were dried up from off the earth.

52 He also sent forth a dove from him, to see if the waters were abated from off the face of the ground; but the dove found no rest for the sole of her foot, and she returned unto him into the ark, for the waters had not receded from off the face of the whole earth; then he put forth his hand and took her, and pulled her in unto him into the ark.

53 And he stayed yet other seven days, and again he sent forth the dove out of the ark, and the dove came in to him in the evening; and lo, in her mouth an olive leaf plucked off; so Noah knew that the waters were abated from off the earth.

54 And he stayed yet other seven days, and sent forth a dove, which returned not again unto him any more.

55 And it came to pass, in the six hundred and first year, in the first month, the first day of the month, the waters were dried up from off the earth.

56 And Noah removed the covering of the ark, and looked, and behold, the face of the ground was dry. And in the second month, on the seven and twentieth day of the month, was the earth dried.

CHAPTER 9

Noah builds an altar -Commandment to not shed blood --
God's covenant, the token of it set in the clouds -- Noah's folly,
the results of it.

1 And God spake unto Noah, saying, Go forth out of the ark, thou and thy wife, and thy sons, and thy sons' wives with thee.

2 Bring forth with thee every living thing that is with thee, of all flesh, both of fowl, and of cattle, and of every creeping thing that creepeth upon the earth; that they may breed abundantly in the earth, and be fruitful and multiply upon the earth.

3 And Noah went forth, and his sons, and his wife, and his sons' wives with him. And every beast, every creeping thing, and every fowl upon the earth, after their kinds, went forth out of the ark.

4 And Noah builded an altar unto the Lord, and took of every clean beast, and of every clean fowl, and offered burnt offerings on the altar; and gave thanks unto the Lord, and rejoiced in his heart.

5 And the Lord spake unto Noah, and he blessed him. And Noah smelled a sweet savor, and he said in his heart;

6 I will call on the name of the Lord, that he will not again curse the ground any more for man's sake, for the imagination of man's heart is evil from his youth; and that he will not again smite any more every thing living, as he hath done, while the earth remaineth;

7 And, that seed-time and harvest, and cold and heat, and summer and winter, and day and night, may not cease with man.

8 And God blessed Noah and his sons, and said unto them, Be fruitful and multiply, and replenish the earth. And the fear of you, and the dread of you shall be upon every beast of the earth, and upon every fowl of the air, upon all that moveth upon the earth, and upon all the fishes of the sea; into your hand are they delivered.

9 Every moving thing that liveth shall be meat for you; even as the green herb have I given you all things.

10 But, the blood of all flesh which I have given you for meat, shall be shed upon the ground, which taketh life thereof, and the blood ye shall not eat.

11 And surely, blood shall not be shed, only for meat, to save your lives; and the blood of every beast will I require at your hands.

12 And whoso sheddeth man's blood, by man shall his blood be shed; for man shall not shed the blood of man.

13 For a commandment I give, that every man's brother shall preserve the life of man, for in mine own image have I made man.

14 And a commandment I give unto you, Be ye fruitful and multiply; bring forth abundantly on the earth, and multiply therein.

15 And God spake unto Noah, and to his sons with him, saying, And I, behold, I will establish my covenant with you, which I made unto your father Enoch, concerning your seed after you.

16 And it shall come to pass, that every living creature that is with you, of the fowl, and of the cattle, and of the beast of the earth that is with you, which shall go out of the ark, shall not altogether perish; neither shall all flesh be cut off any more by the waters of a flood; neither shall there any more be a flood to destroy the earth.

17 And I will establish my covenant with you, which I made unto Enoch, concerning the remnants of your posterity.

18 And God made a covenant with Noah, and said, This shall be the token of the covenant I make between me and you, and for every living creature with you, for perpetual generations;

19 I will set my bow in the cloud; and it shall be for a token of a covenant between me and the earth.

20 And it shall come to pass, when I bring a cloud over the earth, that the bow shall be seen in the cloud; and I will remember my covenant, which I have made between me and you, for every living creature of all flesh. And the waters shall no more become a flood to destroy all flesh.

21 And the bow shall be in the cloud; and I will look upon it, that I may remember the everlasting covenant, which I made unto thy father Enoch; that, when men should keep all my commandments, Zion should again come on the earth, the city of Enoch which I have caught up unto myself.

22 And this is mine everlasting covenant, that when thy posterity shall embrace the truth, and look upward, then shall Zion look downward, and all the heavens shall shake with gladness, and the earth shall tremble with joy;

23 And the general assembly of the church of the firstborn shall come down out of heaven, and possess the earth, and shall have place until the end come. And this is mine everlasting covenant, which I made with thy father Enoch.

24 And the bow shall be in the cloud, and I will establish my covenant unto thee, which I have made between me and thee, for every living creature of all flesh that shall be upon the earth.

25 And God said unto Noah, This is the token of the covenant which I have established between me and thee; for all flesh that shall be upon the earth.

26 And the sons of Noah that went forth of the ark, were Shem, and Ham, and Japheth; and Ham was the father of Canaan. These were the three sons of Noah, and of them was the whole earth overspread.

27 And Noah began to till the earth, and he was an husbandman; and he planted a vineyard, and he drank of the wine, and was drunken; and he was uncovered within his tent;

28 And Ham, the father of Canaan, saw the nakedness of his father, and told his brethren without; and Shem and Japheth took a garment and laid upon both their shoulders, and went backward and covered the nakedness of their father, and they saw not their father's nakedness.

29 And Noah awoke from his wine, and knew what his youngest son had done unto him, and he said, Cursed be Canaan; a servant of servants shall he be unto his brethren.

30 And he said, Blessed be the Lord God of Shem; and Canaan shall be his servant, and a veil of darkness shall cover him, that he shall be known among all men.

31 God shall enlarge Japheth, and he shall dwell in the tents of Shem; and Canaan shall be his servant.

32 And Noah lived after the flood, three hundred and fifty years. **And all the days of Noah were nine hundred and fifty years; and he died.**

...

GENESIS, CHAPTER 11

Babel built – Language confounded -- Generations of Shem -- Abram born; married, and goes into Canaan.

1 And the whole earth* was of the same language, and of the same speech. And it came to pass, that many journeyed from

the east, and as they journeyed from the east, they found a plain in the land of Shinar, and dwelt there in the plain of Shinar. *(Ddd: i.e., likely the part of the only world they knew)*

2 And they said one to another, Come, go to, let us make brick, and burn them thoroughly. And they had brick for stone, and they had slime for mortar.

3 And they said, Come, go to, let us build us a city, and a tower whose top will be high, nigh unto heaven; and let us make us a name, lest we be scattered abroad upon the face of the whole earth.

4 And the Lord came down, beholding the city and the tower which the children of men were building;

5 And the Lord said, Behold, the people are the same, and they all have the same language; and this tower they begin to build, and now, nothing will be restrained from them, which they have imagined, except I, the Lord, confound their language, that they may not understand one another's speech. So I, the Lord, will scatter them abroad from thence, upon all the face of the land, and unto every quarter of the earth.

6 And they were confounded, and left off to build the city, and they hearkened not unto the Lord, therefore, is the name of it called Babel, because the Lord was displeased with their works, and did there confound the language of all the earth; and from thence did the Lord scatter them abroad upon the face thereof.

7 And these were the generations of Shem. **And Shem being an hundred years old, begat Arphaxad two years after the flood**; and Shem lived after he begat Arphaxad five hundred years, and begat sons and daughters.
(Ddd note: 100 + 500 = 600)

8 And **Arphaxad lived five and thirty years, and begat Salah**; and **Arphaxad lived after he begat Salah, four hundred and three years**, and begat sons and daughters.
(Ddd note: 35 + 403 = 438)

9 And **Salah lived thirty years, and begat Eber**; and **Salah lived after he begat Eber four hundred and three years,** and begat sons and daughters.

(Ddd note: 30 + 403 = 433)

10 And **Eber lived four and thirty years, and begat Peleg**; and **Eber lived after he begat Peleg four hundred and thirty years,** and begat sons and daughters.

(Ddd note: 34 + 430 = 464)

11 And **Peleg lived thirty years, and begat Reu**; and **Peleg lived after he begat Reu, two hundred and nine years,** and begat sons and daughters.

(Ddd note: 30 + 209 = 239)

12 **And Reu lived two and thirty years, and begat Serug**; and **Reu lived after he begat Serug two hundred and seven years**, and begat sons and daughters.

(Ddd note: 32 + 207 = 239)

13 And **Serug lived thirty years, and begat Nahor**; and **Serug lived after he begat Nahor two hundred years**, and begat sons and daughters.

(Ddd note: 30 + 200 = 230)

14 And **Nahor lived nine and twenty years, and begat Terah**; and **Nahor lived after he begat Terah and hundred and nineteen years,** and begat sons and daughters.

(Ddd note: 29 + 119 = 148)

15 And **Terah lived seventy years, and begat Abram,** Nahor and Haran.

(Ddd note: The IV departs from the KJV and separates Noah's "triplets" being born in separate years (see Gen. 7:85), but Terah's "triplets" in the IV are not).

16 Now these were the generations of Terah; Terah begat Abram, Nahor and Haran; and Haran begat Lot.

17 And Haran died before his father Terah, in the land of his nativity, in Ur of the Chaldees.

18 And Abram and Nahor took them wives; and the name of Abram's wife was Sarai; and the name of Nahor's wife,

Milcah, the daughter of Haran, the father of Milcah and the father of Iscah; but Sarai was barren, and she bear no child.

19 And Terah took Abram his son, and Lot the son of Haran, his son's son, and Sarai his daughter-in-law, his son Abram's wife; and went forth with them from Ur of the Chaldees, to go into the land of Canaan; and they came unto Haran, and dwelt there.

20 **And the days of Terah were two hundred and five years**; and Terah died in Haran.

GENESIS, CHAPTER 12

God's command to Abram -- He by faith obeys -- Covenant with Abram - Pharaoh plagued for Sarai's sake.

1 **Now,** the Lord had said unto Abram, **Get thee out of thy country,** and from thy kindred, and from thy father's house, unto a land that I will show thee;

2 And I will make of thee a great nation, and I will bless thee, and make thy name great; and thou shalt be a blessing; and I will bless them that bless thee, and curse them that curse thee; and in thee shall the families of the earth be blessed.

3 So Abram departed, as the Lord had spoken unto him; and Lot went with him. And **Abram was seventy and five years old when he departed out of Haran.**

*(Ddd note: Scriptural error. This verse conflicts with **Gen. 11:15 (JST)** which lists Abram **first** of three sons born to Terah, when Terah was 70 years old; indicating Abram to be the senior and the first to be born, hence the oldest. If Terah was 205 when he died and in the self-same year Abram left Haran and he was 75 at that time, then Terah was 130 when he begat Abram and not 70 [205-75=130]. Otherwise, Abram was 135 when Terah died and not 75 [205-135=70]. Ussher chooses Terah to be 130 when he begat Abram, Doddridge chooses 70. The only effect of this is about a 2.2 years average reduction in period 7 from 37.04 to 34.81 years average.)*

...

GENESIS, CHAPTER 14

...

25 And Melchizedek lifted up his voice and blessed Abram.

26 Now Melchizedek was a man of faith, who wrought righteousness; and when a child he feared God, and stopped the mouths of lions, and quenched the violence of fire.

27 And thus, having been approved of God, he was ordained an high priest after the order of the covenant which God made with Enoch,

28 It being after the order of the Son of God; which order came, not by man, nor the will of man; neither by father nor mother; neither by beginning of days nor end of years; but of God;

29 And it was delivered unto men by the calling of his own voice, according to his own will, unto as many as believed on his name.

30 For God having sworn unto Enoch and unto his seed with an oath by himself; that every one being ordained after this order and calling should have power, by faith, to break mountains, to divide the seas, to dry up waters, to turn them out of their course;

31 To put at defiance the armies of nations, to divide the earth, to break every band, to stand in the presence of God; to do all things according to his will, according to his command, subdue principalities and powers; and this by the will of the Son of God which was from before the foundation of the world.

32 And men having this faith, coming up unto this order of God, were translated and taken up into heaven.

33 And now, Melchizedek was a priest of this order; therefore he obtained peace in Salem, and was called the Prince of peace.

34 And his people wrought righteousness, and obtained heaven, and sought for the city of Enoch which God had before taken, separating it from the earth, having reserved it unto the latter days, or the end of the world;

35 And hath said, and sworn with an oath, that the heavens and the earth should come together; and the sons of God should be tried so as by fire.

36 And this Melchizedek, having thus established righteousness, was called the king of heaven by his people, or, in other words, the King of peace.
37 And he lifted up his voice, and he blessed Abram, being the high priest, and the keeper of the storehouse of God;
38 Him whom God had appointed to receive tithes for the poor.
39 Wherefore, Abram paid unto him tithes of all that he had, of all the riches which he possessed, which God had given him more than that which he had need.
40 And it came to pass, that God blessed Abram, and gave unto him riches, and honor, and lands for an everlasting possession; according to the covenant which he had made, and according to the blessing wherewith Melchizedek had blessed him.

...

CHAPTER 15

God covenants with Abram -- Abram's vision -- The captivity foretold.

1 And it came to pass, that after these things, the word of the Lord came unto Abram in a vision, saying;
2 Fear not, Abram; I will be thy shield; I will be thy exceeding great reward. And according to the blessings of my servant, I will give unto thee.
3 And Abram said, Lord God, what wilt thou give me, seeing I go childless, and Eliezer of Damascus was made the steward of my house?
4 And Abram said, Behold, to me thou hast given no seed; and lo, one born in my house is mine heir.
5 And behold, the word of the Lord came unto him again, saying,
6 This shalt not be thine heir; but he that shall come forth out of thine own bowels shall be thine heir.
7 And he brought him forth abroad, and he said, Look now toward heaven, and tell the stars, if thou be able to number them.
8 And he said unto him, so shall thy seed be.

9 And Abram said, Lord God, how wilt thou give me this land for an everlasting inheritance?

10 And the Lord said, Though thou wast dead, yet am I not able to give it thee?

11 And if thou shalt die, yet thou shalt possess it, for the day cometh, that the Son of Man shall live; but how can he live if he be not dead? he must first be quickened.

12 And it came to pass that Abram looked forth and saw the days of the Son of Man, and was glad, and his soul found rest, and he believed in the Lord; and the Lord counted it unto him for righteousness.

13 And the Lord said unto him, I, the Lord, brought thee out of Ur, of the Chaldees, to give thee this land to inherit it.

14 And Abram said, Lord, whereby shall I know that I shall inherit it? yet he believed God. And the Lord said unto him, Take me a heifer of three years old, and a she goat of three years old, and a ram of three years old, and a turtle-dove, and a young pigeon.

15 And he took unto him all these, and he divided them in the midst, and he laid each piece one against the other; but the birds divided he not.

16 And when the fowls came down upon the carcasses, Abram drove them away. And when the sun was going down, a deep sleep fell upon Abram; and, lo, a great horror of darkness fell upon him. 17 And the Lord spake, and he said unto Abram, Know of a surety that **Thy seed shall be a stranger in a land which shall not be theirs, and shall serve strangers; and they shall be afflicted, and serve them four hundred years**; and also that nation whom they shall serve will I judge; and afterwards shall they come out with great substance.

18 And thou shalt die, and go to thy fathers in peace; thou shalt be buried in a good old age.

19 But in the fourth generation they shall come hither again; for the iniquity of the Amorites is not yet full.

20 And it came to pass, that when the sun went down, and it was dark, behold, a smoking furnace, and a burning lamp which passed between those pieces which Abram had divided.

21 And in that same day the Lord made a covenant with Abram, saying, **Unto thy seed have I given this land, from the river of Egypt unto the great river Euphrates;**
22 The Kenites, and the Kenazites, and the Kadmonites, and Hittites, and the Perizzites, and the Rephaims, and the Amorites, and the Canaanites, and the Girgashites, and the Jebusites.
...

GENESIS, CHAPTER 21

A son born to Abraham – Isaac named -- Bondwoman cast out -Covenant with Abimelech.

1 And the Lord visited Sarah as he had said, and the Lord did unto Sarah as he had spoken by the mouth of his angels; for Sarah conceived and bear Abraham a son in his old age, at the set time of which the angels of God had spoken to him.
2 And Abraham called the name of his son that was born unto him, whom Sarah bear unto him, Isaac.
3 And Abraham circumcised his son Isaac, he being eight days old, as God had commanded him.
4 **And Abraham was an hundred years old, when his son Isaac was born unto him.**
5 And Sarah said, God has made me to rejoice; and also all that know me will rejoice with me.
6 And she said unto Abraham, Who would have said that Sarah should have given children suck? For I was barren, but the Lord promised, and I have borne unto Abraham a son in his old age.
...

GENESIS, CHAPTER 25

Abraham marrieth Keturah – His death -- The generations of Ishmael -- His death -- The birth of Esau and Jacob -- Esau selleth his birthright.

1 Then again Abraham took a wife, and her name was Keturah.
2 And she bare him Zimran, and Jokshan, and Medan, and Midian, and Ishbak, and Shuah.

3 And Jokshan begat Sheba, and Dedan. And the sons of Dedan were Asshurim, and Letushim, and Leummim.

4 And the sons of Midian; Ephah, and Epher, and Hanoch, and Abidah, and Eldaah. All these were the children of Keturah.

5 And Abraham gave all that he had unto Isaac.

6 But unto the sons of the concubines, which Abraham had, Abraham gave gifts, and sent them away from Isaac his son, while he yet lived, eastward, unto the east country.

7 And these are the number of the years of Abraham's life, which he lived, a hundred threescore and fifteen years.

8 Then Abraham gave up the ghost, and died in a good old age, an old man, and full of years; and was gathered to his people.

9 And his sons Isaac and Ishmael buried him in the cave of Machpelah, in the field of Ephron the son of Zohar the Hittite, which is before Mamre;

...

19 And these are the generations of Isaac, Abraham's son; Abraham begat Isaac;

20 And Isaac was forty years old when he took Rebekah to wife, the daughter of Bethuel the Syrian of Padan-aram, the sister to Laban the Syrian.

21 And Isaac entreated the Lord for his wife, that she might bare children, because she was barren. And the Lord was entreated of him, and Rebekah his wife conceived.

22 And the children struggled together within her womb; and she said, If I am with child, why is it thus with me? And she went to inquire of the Lord.

23 And the Lord said unto her, Two nations are in thy womb, and two manner of people shall be separated from thy bowels; and the one people shall be stronger than the other people; and the elder shall serve the younger.

24 And when her days to be delivered were fulfilled, behold, there were twins in her womb.

25 And the first came out red, all over like a hairy garment; and they called his name Esau.

26 And after that came his brother out, and his hand took hold on Esau's heel; and **his name was called Jacob; and Isaac was threescore years old when she bare them.**

27 And the boys grew; and Esau was a cunning hunter, a man of the field; and Jacob was a plain man, dwelling in tents.

28 And Isaac loved Esau, because he did eat of his venison; but Rebekah loved Jacob.

29 And Jacob sod pottage; and Esau came from the field, and he was faint;

30 And Esau said to Jacob, Feed me, I pray thee, with that same red pottage; for I am faint; therefore was his name called Edom.

31 And Jacob said, Sell me this day thy birthright.

32 And Esau said, Behold, I am at the point of dying; and what shall this birthright profit me?

33 And Jacob said, Swear to me this day; and he swore unto him; and he sold his birthright unto Jacob.

34 Then Jacob gave Esau bread and pottage of lentils; and he did eat and drink, and rose up, and went his way. Thus Esau despised his birthright.

...

GENESIS, CHAPTER 35

...

28 And the days of **Isaac were a hundred and fourscore years**.

29 And Isaac gave up the ghost, and died, and was gathered unto his people, being old and full of days; and his sons Esau and Jacob buried him.

...

GENESIS, CHAPTER 47

...

28 And Jacob lived in the land of Egypt seventeen years: so **the whole age of Jacob was an hundred forty and seven years.**

...

LUKE 3:38 in KJV, (3:45 in JST)
(King James Version, verse 38, compared with Joseph Smith Translation, same verse, is verse 45 in JST)

...

38 Which was *the son* of Enos, which was *the son* of Seth, which was *the son* of **Adam, which was *the son* of God.** *(KJV; ba)*

45 And of Enos, and of Seth, and of **Adam, who was formed of God, and the first man upon the earth.** *(JST; ba)*

~~~

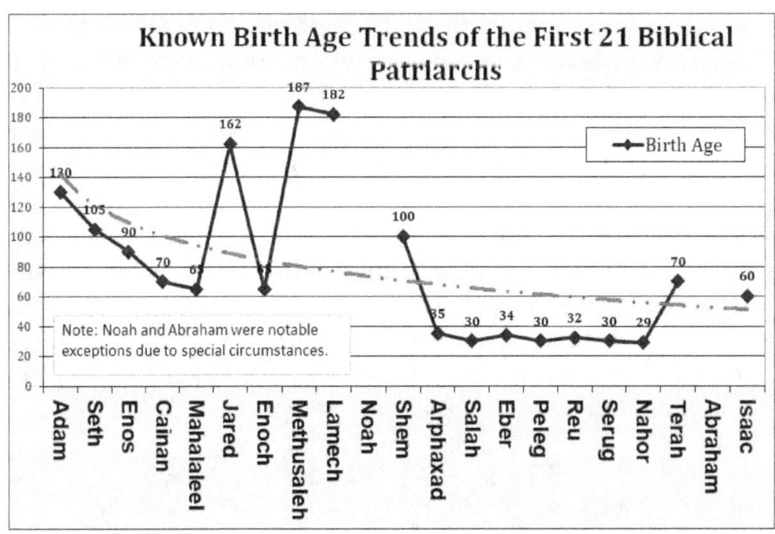
~~~

11. The Doddridge Chronology

The Harmony between Evolution and the Scriptures
Part 1. The beginning of time, the first flesh, Scatterings, the Flood,
Living substance, Cursed is the ground for our sakes.
Part 2. Scriptures and evolution, Adam-ondi-Ahman, Map.
Part 3. Conclusion.

I.

The earlier part of this book evaluates the Doddridge Chronology with the Ussher Chronology, pointing out some important weaknesses of the latter, for example, the starting date of our temporal existence, and which hopefully the Doddridge Chronology remedies.

Basically, after all of the work was done, I saw that Ussher was about 200-300 years off the mark, specifically 264 years. Yet he was convinced that David was born about 1085BC. This then produced a dilemma. With all those extra years to account for, his average age for the firstborn son more than doubled with what the scriptures were showing was a downward trend (ref. p. 163).

Joseph Smith received a revelation about the earth's "temporal existence" of man – revealing that period of time, from beginning to end, was to be **7,000 years**.

Additionally, Joseph Smith received several revelations mentioning that Christ came in the 1,000 year "**meridian of time**." Among the several definitions of the word *meridian* we find in the Webster dictionary, the archaic meaning as "the hour of noon." It also describes it as "**a high point** (as of development or prosperity)." *(Merriam-Webster Dictionary https://www.merriam-webster.com/dictionary/meridian; May2018; ba)*

The high point or middle of the seven millennia is the 4th (3000-4000 year) millennium. In summary of events, Adam began his mortal journey in the 1st millennium, at 3,740BC; the 2nd millennium would be at 2740-1740BC; the 3rd would be 1740-740BC; the 4th at 740BC-260AD; *Christ's birth **in** this "high point" 4th millennium*; the 5th would be 260-1260AD; the 6th Millennium at 1260-2260AD, the 7th final millennium at 2260-3260AD. Modifying the 6th by a 70-year guesstimated 1% "shortening" to end in 2,190AD, and then adding back in the guesstimated 1% 70-year, as a "little season" after the end of the 7th, to release Lucifer, the total would still be 7,000 years.

The Beginning of Time.

As Archbishop Ussher describes the "beginning of time" (see p.104) in his book The Annals of the World, I thought I'd take issue with that offering some of my own thoughts on the subject. I do not adhere to the "young earth" or other such creationist theories, where all life began on the earth only a few thousand years ago (imagine the patriarchs were obligated to defend themselves against dinosaurs and such). Nor do I subscribe to the theory this earth was created from another past earth *with beings having spirits*, that for whatever reason they never went through their own millennium and resurrection.

> 34 And the first man of all men have I called Adam, which is many.
>
> 35 But only an account of this earth, and the inhabitants thereof, give I unto you. For behold, **there are many worlds that have passed away by the word of my power**. And there are many that now stand, and innumerable are they unto man; but all things are numbered unto me, for they are mine and I know them.
>
> 36 And it came to pass that Moses spake unto the Lord, saying: Be merciful unto thy servant, O God, and tell me concerning this earth, and the inhabitants thereof, and also the heavens, and then thy servant will be content.
>
> 37 And the Lord God spake unto Moses, saying: The heavens, they are many, and they cannot be numbered unto man; but they are numbered unto me, for they are mine.
>
> 38 **And as one earth shall pass away, and the heavens thereof even so shall another come**, and there is no end to my works, neither to my words. *(Moses 1:34-38; ba)*

The quote above speaks of God's works triggering *many* earths to pass away, thus they must have afterwards become eternal (see 2Peter 3:10-13). But as every earth inhabited by the sons of God will experience a similar +/- 7000-year temporal existence and thereafter be resurrected, they will not pass away and that be the end of them, but rather the mortality of each will pass away to become an *eternal* celestial planet, and not part of another.

I believe archeologists have quite fully established the processes of evolution and that this earth was occupied by Pre-Adamites (without spirits) before, during, and after the time that Adam and the Garden were placed on the earth in what was once a desolate spot in what is now called Jackson County, Missouri in the United States.

> ... the spot chosen for the garden of Eden was Jackson County, in the State of Missouri, where Independence now stands; it was occupied in the morn of creation by Adam and his associates who came with him for the express purpose of peopling this earth. *(Heber C Kimball, Jun27,1863, JD 10:235; see also p.175,176)*

> If, however, there are some things in the strata of the earth indicating there were men before Adam they were not the ancestors of Adam. *(General Conference, p. 123, Apr 06, 1953, Marion G Romney)*

The first flesh.

Some members of the Church of Jesus Christ of Latter-day Saints who are creationists might oppose Pre-Adamite evidences of life before Adam with a verse in Moses:

> And I, the Lord God, formed man from the dust of the ground, and breathed into his nostrils **the breath of life**; and **man became a living soul, the first flesh upon the earth, the first man also**; nevertheless, all things were before created; but spiritually were they created and made according to my word. *(Moses 3:7)*

We need to read the whole verse however and not just part of it. We know that the act of *breathing into Adam's nostrils* the "breath of life" an organized spirit, is symbolic. The Church has repeatedly over the years by different prophets stated that Adam was created by procreation (see p.188). The whole idea here conveyed is that Adam *became* the "first flesh" and the "first man" *only when* God placed Adam's spirit into his body, thus becoming a "living soul." Beings of evolution have not gotten that far – there is no organized spirit breathed into them, thus they are not qualified to be regarded as flesh or as men in God's terms. This verse only deals with God's creations having souls and not those of evolution. It may seem a mite callous, but Pre-Adamites who have no organized spirit entity are really just extensions of the earth itself. As the Book of Mormon explains what would happen to our bodies if Jesus was not the Christ and the resurrection was not a reality:

> ... this flesh must have laid down to rot and to crumble to its mother earth, to rise no more. *(2 Ne. 9:7)*

Such is the case with beings whose sole ancestors include the Australopithecus and related kin and none from Adam. The Scriptures do not consider them the "first flesh" any more than the earth itself is a first flesh.

The Scatterings.

Indeed, the later scattering of the *chosen* Israelites (direct descendants of Adam with spirits) to the far reaches of the world was part of the original plan, a second stage, to seed the earth with chosen beings having spirits, and by intermarriage replacing those that don't. All of the descendants of Adam have spirits. The result would be a world of beings with spirits through intermarriage. In fact, the earlier scattering of the people at the Tower of Babel, the first stage of scattering, also had the same desired goal.

> 8 So the LORD scattered them abroad from thence upon the face of all the earth: and they left off to build the city.
> 9 Therefore is the name of it called Babel; because the LORD did there confound the language of all the earth: and from thence did the LORD scatter them abroad upon the face of all the earth. *(Gen. 11:8,9)*

The Flood.

The Flood was conducted world-wide to baptize the earth, and to destroy all the seed of Adam and animal life, *wherein there is the breath of life*, i.e. having individual organized spirits made by God. Adam brought animals *with spirits* to this earth also.

> He [Adam] was the person who brought the animals and the seeds from other planets to this world and brought a wife with him and stayed here. You may read and believe what you please as to what is found written in the Bible. Adam was made from the dust of an earth, but not from the dust of this earth. He was made as you and I are made, and no person was ever made upon any other principle. *(JD3:319, Brigham Young, Apr 20, 1856)*

> And, behold, I, even I, do bring a flood of waters upon the earth, to destroy all flesh, **wherein *is* the breath of life**, from under heaven; *and* every thing that *is* in the earth shall die. *(Gen. 6:17)*
> And they went in unto Noah into the ark, two and two of all flesh, **wherein *is* the breath of life**. *(Gen. 7:15)*

Living substance.

Many Pre-Adamites survived the flooding in their parts of the earth, which might have been only a few feet deep. **The scriptural report of the Flood is *only* concerned with *living substance*, i.e. with beings and life with spirits,** and *not with life without organized spirits*, such as trees, plants, insects, parasites, bacteria, vegetation, certain animals, and pre-Adamite humans all of which had evolved over millions of years.

Did Noah take two mayflies into the ark? Did he take two human beings formed from evolution? How about two mosquitos or anything made by evolution? No, they are not even mentioned, being of no concern in the scriptures, nor whether any such life would survive the flood. Anything from evolution has no breath of life, i.e. no *organized living substance or spirit*, that God would recognize as having its roots in the celestial realms. Without an organized spirit, evolutionized life will never be resurrected and go to a heaven.

Technically, being "alive" does not require a union with an *organized* spirit to be inside the body. All spirit element is "alive," that is, it acts as an agent of *composition and decomposition,* regardless of its standing on the wide scale of spirit elements. As most or all physical matter, organized and unorganized, is amalgamated with native spirit element*, really, all or most everything in the universe is alive. Indeed, mortal matter itself may be but a denser form of spirit matter.   * *See Glossary / Spirit.*

> And I knew such a man, (whether in the body, or out of the body, I cannot tell: God knoweth); *(2 Cor. 12:3)*

> And whether they were in the body or out of the body, they could not tell; *(3 Nephi 28:15)*

> THE heavens were opened upon us, and I beheld the celestial kingdom of God, and the glory thereof, whether in the body or out I cannot tell. *(D&C 137:1)*

These three scriptures attest to prophets wondering whether they – that is their spirits – had left their still living bodies for a time. Obviously, they thought it possible that their bodies would continue to be living while their spirits were gone off to heaven or someplace else.

> For as the body without the spirit is dead, ... *(James 2:26)*

James here was referring to the *human* body separating from an *organized* spirit (having an intelligence). Separating the body from the organized spirit equates death *for the soul.*

But, should we also assume every living microorganism, virus and parasite, every plant that does and ever has existed, every evolutionized being had an organized individual spirit and will be resurrected? Heaven forbid! Yet they are/were alive without organized spirits.

The mortal body has no eternal existence without an organized spirit assigned to it.

> ... the spirit indeed *is* willing, but the flesh *is* weak. *(Matt.26:41; note that the flesh, a functioning and living organism, has a will, one independent of the spirit, albeit weaker than a spirit. But all matter has (or is) spirit, organized or unorganized, else it would certainly be dead)*

A spirit normally joins its mortal body while the latter is a growing fetus in the womb. Similarly, can a spirit join to a person from evolution, say, if they became converted to the true Gospel? I do not think *only* in the womb can a spirit enter and possess a mortal body and become a permanent part of it. That is possibly one reason why devils attempt it. Consider also the effect of the Holy Ghost upon a convert who is a "Gentile."

> … the effect of the Holy Ghost upon a Gentile, is to purge out the old blood, and make him actually of the seed of Abraham." *(Joseph Smith, DHC 3:380)*

I suppose it is not unreasonable to suggest that *if* the converted "Gentile" were a person of evolution origin, the Holy Ghost would quicken the person at that same time with an organized spirit. Needless to say, that person with a new individual spirit in his/her body would have a "mighty change of heart" (see Alma 5:14)!

Cursed is the ground *for our sake*.

A question naturally arises, why did the gods place Adam here on *this* earth of all places, if it was already moderately populated with beings produced from evolution having no spirits? Interesting is the fact that evolution will eventually and always develop beings that are compatible through intermarriage with the sons of God. In fact, they are vital to the eternal plan as we shall see. The answer is that when Adam left the Garden, he was still nearly completely immortal with only a tad of mortality in his veins introduced from eating a sampling of "forbidden" fruit. He was not yet subject to illness, injury, and all of the misery associated with mortal beings. But he was promised:

> 17 And unto Adam he said, Because thou hast hearkened unto the voice of thy wife, and hast eaten of the tree, of which I commanded thee, saying, Thou shalt not eat of it: **cursed *is* the ground for thy sake**; in sorrow shalt thou eat *of* it all the days of thy life;
>
> 18 Thorns also and thistles shall it bring forth to thee; and thou shalt eat the herb of the field;
>
> 19 In the sweat of thy face shalt thou eat bread, till thou return unto the ground; for out of it wast thou taken: for

dust thou *art,* and unto dust shalt thou return. *(Gen. 3:17-19)*

Obviously, God *wanted* Adam *and his seed* to have hardships, trials, travails and tribulations. But why?

11 **For it must needs be, that there is an opposition in all things**. If not so, my first-born in the wilderness, righteousness could not be brought to pass, neither wickedness, neither holiness nor misery, neither good nor bad. Wherefore, all things must needs be a compound in one; wherefore, if it should be one body it must needs remain as dead, having no life neither death, nor corruption nor incorruption, happiness nor misery, neither sense nor insensibility.

12 Wherefore, it must needs have been created for a thing of naught; **wherefore there would have been no purpose in the end of its creation**. Wherefore, this thing must needs destroy the wisdom of God and his eternal purposes, and also the power, and the mercy, and the justice of God.

13 And if ye shall say there is no law, ye shall also say there is no sin. If ye shall say there is no sin, ye shall also say there is no righteousness. And if there be no righteousness there be no happiness. And if there be no righteousness nor happiness there be no punishment nor misery. And if these things are not there is no God. And if there is no God we are not, neither the earth; for there could have been no creation of things, neither to act nor to be acted upon; wherefore, all things must have vanished away.

14 And now, my sons, I speak unto you these things for your profit and learning; for there is a God, and he hath created all things, both the heavens and the earth, and all things that in them are, both things to act and things to be acted upon.

15 And to bring about his eternal purposes in the end of man, after he had created our first parents, and the beasts of the field and the fowls of the air, and in fine, all things which are created, it must needs be that there was an opposition; even the forbidden fruit in opposition to the tree of life; the one being sweet and the other bitter.

> 16 Wherefore, the Lord God gave unto man that he should act for himself. Wherefore, man could not act for himself save it should be that he was enticed by the one or the other. *(2 Nephi 2:11-16; ba)*

II.

Scriptures and evolution.

The beings from evolution were rife with all manner of mortal diseases and weaknesses that Adam and his posterity did not have. The sons of God, Adam's seed, married the daughters of men (of evolution), thereby integrating their pains and ailments into their more immortal offspring from their mortal genetics, diets and staples. This resulted in a lowering of their children's longevity and increasing the climate *for testing and solidifying of virtues.* And now we perceive a major reason for evolution, of life produced by lower forms of spirit element scattered over the universe, mixing with mortal matter, and allowed by God to evolve. Evolution and mortal substance create humans without organized spirits, but compatible with the descendants of Adam, to subject those descendants to all manner of disease and other disorders infused into their partially immortal bodies and into their children. These weaknesses and infirmities then become *a deliberate and planned testing ground* to subject the sons and daughters of the gods to overcome in an "opposition in all things" environment. Without evolutionized beings and mortal substance, the mortalization process of immortal persons would be more difficult as their partially immortal bodies might likely reject most infirmities without an ancillary gene pool from the Pre-Adamites. Thus, each of us in this mortal life will be subject to sorrows, sickness, misery and so on. Our Eternal Father may be motivated by our righteousness to *temper* our woes or even *heal* us on occasion but otherwise will not remove them. As Christ prayed:

> 42 Saying, Father, if thou be willing, remove this cup from me: nevertheless not my will, but thine, be done.

43 And there appeared an angel unto him from heaven, strengthening him. *(Luke 22:42, 43)*

In our own mortal and far less worthy experience that will ultimately end in our deaths, we may not get relief from an angelic visitation as Christ did, but God's spirit may provide moral support while we persevere and endure unto the end. These evolutionized beings are not directly addressed anywhere in the scriptures, except possibly through inference in a few isolated verses. Examples include when the sons of God married the daughters of men – those from evolution; or by default when He wishes to make a qualified distinction of the organized life He placed on the earth as in Genesis 7:4 from living substance that He did not directly make (see below).

> AND it came to pass, when men began to multiply on the face of the earth, and daughters were born unto them,
>
> 2 That the sons of God [descendants of Adam] saw the daughters of men [descended from evolution] that they *were* fair; and they took them wives of all which they chose.
>
> 3 And the LORD said, My spirit shall not always strive with man, for that he also *is* flesh: yet his days shall be an hundred and twenty years.
>
> 4 There were **giants in the earth in those days**; and also after that, when the sons of God came in unto the daughters of men, and **they bare *children* to them, the same became mighty men** which *were* of old, men of renown. *(Gen. 6:2-4; [ ] added; ba; also see JST, Gen. 8:6-9)*
>
> ... and every living substance **that I have made*** will I destroy from off the face of the earth. *(Gen. 7:4 [Gen.8:32 JST]; ba; * as distinct from those evolution made (or He is accentuating He made every "living" substance, i.e., those that have souls).)*
>
> And he cometh into the world that he may save all men if they will hearken unto his voice; for behold, he suffereth the pains of all men, yea, the pains of every living creature, both men, women, and children, **who belong to the family of Adam****. *(2 Ne. 9:21; ** as distinct from those who do not belong to the family of Adam)*

Ussher believed the "men" during the time of Seth and Enos were apostates of Adam's seed (p.108). Many of them undoubtedly were. I can imagine that Cain, Abel, Adam and Eve and ensuing children had already encountered natives in Missouri not too long after the Garden was removed. They interacted with one another and trade began. Different religious beliefs from the natives were encountered and embraced by some. Marriages took place. Sometimes giants resulted by combining immortal elements from one spouse with the mortal elements of the other spouse.

God took a dim look at such marriages *when* the non-chosen from evolution and apostates seduced His chosen seed to wickedness and idolatry. Note that Terah, 19th patriarch from Adam, was a polytheist *(Joshua 24:2)*. Otherwise, God desired that his chosen seed would be mixed with all of the world's peoples to have them recognize Him as the true God, to be "fruitful and multiply" *(Gen. 1:28)*, producing innumerable children having spirits, and to join the elect.

Adam-ondi-Ahman.

Even up to the time of Noah, Adam's seed was still fenced in to the American continents by oceans, seas, and ice. *That was the whole world to them*. Europe, Africa, Asia, Australia, the islands were not known to them, except perhaps by revelation; and all of the evolution-humans on those continents were likely in the millions.

> 19 And the waters prevailed exceedingly upon the earth; and all the high hills, that *were* under the whole heaven, were covered.
>
> 20 **Fifteen cubits upward** did the waters prevail; and the mountains were covered [29].

---

[29] Note the Scripture does not say Mt. Everest was covered by 22.5 feet of water – only that the 15 cubits of water resulted in covering the mountains to an unknown depth, perhaps even by snow or thorough drenchings. Likely there could have been tsunamis on the plains of Olaha Shinehah (see p.176), and elsewhere throughout the world to assure no survivors of persons "wherein there was the breath of life" (individuals with spirits). As the Americas were

21 And all flesh died that moved upon the earth, both of fowl, and of cattle, and of beast, and of every creeping thing that creepeth upon the earth, and every man:
22 **All in whose nostrils *was* the breath of life, of all that *was* in the dry *land,* died**.
23 And every living substance was destroyed which was upon the face of the ground, both man, and cattle, and the creeping things, and the fowl of the heaven; and they were destroyed from the earth: and Noah only remained *alive,* and they that *were* with him in the ark.
24 And the waters prevailed upon the earth an hundred and fifty days. *(Gen. 7:19-23)*

Notice the scriptures remind us the intent of the flood was to kill all things *alive that had souls*, i.e., organized spirits or the "breath of life" (see p. 86, 168).

How high was the flood waters? 15 cubits or more. Consensus has it that a cubit is 18 inches, the typical length of an arm. 15 x 18" = 22.5 feet. If it covered the mountains, then the mountains were not very high – but it did. Trees grow to heights taller than that. Buildings are built higher than that, maybe even back then. Taum Sauk Mountain in Missouri, around 200+ miles from Adam-ondi-Ahman, where Noah likely lived at the time, today stands at 1,772 feet elevation. How high was it 3,862 years ago in the flood? I would imagine it was still as tall or thereabouts.

We can properly conclude that in the plains of Olaha Shinehah (see quotes below), the flood waters were deeper, enough so that the Ark would have been lifted well above the ground. Sailing south it would have eventually reached the ocean, and then on to Asia where it landed about five months later. They then began renaming rivers and geographical points after the same names they used in America. I wonder

---

isolated from the rest of the world, it is highly unlikely that any of Adam's descendants succeeded in emigrating to the other continents in those primitive times – until Noah.

if they even knew they were no longer in Missouri – just a thought. Of course, they did.

52 Noah was ten years old when he was ordained under the hand of Methuselah.

53 Three years previous to the death of Adam, he called Seth, Enos, Cainan, Mahalaleel, Jared, Enoch, and Methuselah, who were all high priests, with the residue of his posterity who were righteous, into the valley of Adam-ondi-Ahman, and there bestowed upon them his last blessing.

54 And the Lord appeared unto them, and they rose up and blessed Adam, and called him Michael, the prince, the archangel. *(D&C 107:52-54)*

Revelation given to Joseph Smith the Prophet, near Wight's Ferry, at a place called Spring Hill, Daviess County, Missouri, May 19, 1838, wherein Spring Hill is named by the Lord; ADAM-ONDI-AHMAN, because said he, it is the place where Adam shall come to visit his people, or the Ancient of Days shall sit, as spoken of by Daniel the prophet. (D&C 116:1; from 1968 version. Note: later versions changed the wording a little; DHC 3:35)

Is there not room enough **on the mountains of Adam-ondi-Ahman, and on the plains of Olaha Shinehah**, or the land where Adam dwelt, ... *(D&C 117:8; ba)*

The "mountains" of Daviess County, Missouri (if anything there can be claimed to be a mountain) today rise to an elevation of little more than 1000 feet. But some miles to the east today is the 703-acre Thousand Hills State Park, elevation 814 ft. This was the world to Noah. He might have wandered away from this area to other parts of the American continents during his lifetime, perhaps to visit kin who had migrated elsewhere and had intermarried with those from evolution. But in the years leading up to the flood, Methuselah and Lamech, aged men then, would most likely have stayed in or around Adam-ondi-Ahman. No doubt Noah also would have lived around his ancestor's home. Noah would have gathered specimens from all of the animals there, who had organized spirits, all descended from the animals that Adam added to the earth when he came to settle there.

How about the Himalayas and other such ranges far away, lands wholly unknown to Noah except perhaps by vision? Snow, a form of water would likely have been the means to cover them with water. In toto, the earth's land masses would have been all covered with water, if even only an inch or two soaking, for the completion of the earth's baptism at some point during the 150 days of the flood.

> And the waters prevailed upon the earth an hundred and fifty days. *(Gen.7:24)*

There were no African elephants or other Old World animals that swam the Atlantic to join themselves with Noah and the Ark. At any rate, the Ark was restricted to beings and animals with organized spirits, all of which originally came with Adam. It was only after the Flood, that the Ark landed in Asia or thereabouts. There were resurrected animals – *likely* elephants, horses, and other species from the immortal realms, that Adam brought in his interplanetary ark to mate with their evolutionized counterparts elsewhere in the world (see p.168). Makes sense. Bring this earth to higher levels of existence. Elephants and horses, etc., having organized spirits, descendants of the resurrected ones that Adam brought, on Noah's ark. After it landed in Asia, they were released to mate with those of evolution.

Why elephants and horses of all animals to mention here?

> 19 And out of the ground the LORD God formed every **beast of the field**, and every **fowl of the air**; and brought *them* unto Adam to see what he would call them: and whatsoever Adam called every living creature, that *was* the name thereof.
>
> 20 And Adam gave names to all **cattle**, and to the **fowl of the air**, and to every **beast of the field**; but for Adam there was not found an help meet for him. *(Gen. 2:19,20)*

As we can see, Adam did not rename every animal on the planet, but rather only those that he brought with him. Only "beasts of the field" are listed in the Bible – those animals like cattle, horses, and maybe even elephants and other beasts that can work the fields and be a help for human agrarian assistance. Fowl of the air are also mentioned – doves, pigeons, maybe even chickens, etc.

Were there other immortal animals (with spirits) that were also brought, but not revealed? Surely, yes. It is reasonable to assume that dogs, cats, even honeybees[30], and a whole array of other animals with organized spirits (but without godlike intelligences) were brought here with Adam's ark too. Then samples of these were loaded into Noah's ark.

After Noah's Ark landed in Asia, Ham and Egyptus migrated to Africa, where their sons and daughters with spirits began intermarrying with the non-spirit peoples there. And the same with Shem and Japheth, where they went, to Asia, Europe, and so on. As they intermarried, those populations would become possessed of organized spirits as well. As time progressed, the "chosen" blood of Adam began to fully permeate the world's populations.

For the record, *Pangaea*, an ancient continent where most the world's land masses were then in one location, divided some 200 million years ago, and *not a few thousand years ago* when the *nations* were created in the days of Peleg as some have claimed.

> Gen. 10:25 ...the name of one *was* Peleg; for in his days was the earth divided; ... *(This verse speaks only of political or national divisions, see Gen. 10:32 next)*
>
> Gen. 10:32 These *are* the families of the sons of Noah, after their generations, in their nations: and by these were the nations divided in the earth after the flood.

---

[30] After the Flood, the Brother of Jared and company brought "deseret" (honeybees) with them back to America, obviously because they had been wiped out earlier from the Flood as part of those animals that had "the breath of life" in them (see Ether 2:3). Hence Michael must have brought them with him when he came to earth from the celestial realms.

Noah's Journey Map

III.

Today, there are no longer any races, cultures, peoples, tribes, persons, etc. remaining anywhere on earth without spirits that are solely descended from Pre-Adamites. The blood of Adam has now reached even into the remotest jungles of Africa, in Asia and elsewhere. All can claim ancestry to Adam. All humans today now have organized spirits.[31] All can now receive the Priesthood, be sealed, and go on to an eternal exaltation.

> And hath made of one blood all nations of men for to dwell on all the face of the earth, and hath determined the times before appointed, and the bounds of their habitation; *(Acts17:26)*

In summary, when we factor in

- o the realities and evidences of the existence of evolution on this planet, along with reliable dating methods, and that they should not be ignored when studying mankind's true history, and that the scriptural accounts of the Flood are also true;
- o that we are partly descended from beings produced by evolution, inheriting their infirmities and weaknesses; and partly descended from the gods with their greater strengths and eternal capacity;
- o that Pangaea (when the continents were one land) actually broke apart some 175-200 million years before Peleg and not just a few thousand years ago;
- o that Adam and the Garden were founded in Missouri;
- o Noah would have resided only in the Americas and not have been a globetrotter;

---

[31] Each organized human spirit is first composed of spirit element and an intelligence organized in the womb of a Heavenly Mother, before their birth in the heavens. *Before organizing with a spirit fetus*, eternal intelligences are not dormant. Assisting the universal powers, they *may* integrate with evolutionized beings promoting the processes of evolution until the evolving beings die, and then reincarnate again with others, until it is their turn to become part of a new, organizing spirit fetus. See also Glossary: Intelligence; Spirit; Organized Spirit.

- o the realization that Noah would not have found a way to voyage from the Americas to all the other world's continents during those primitive years (Though some studies *suggest* that ocean travel by the Polynesians was accomplished up to 10,000 years ago – 4,500 years before Adam); hence
- o Noah would not have had the means of bringing animals over to his construction site in the Americas from *all* over the world without *first* already having an ark-sized ship to pick them up;

we begin to realize that introducing authenticity into the world's chronology and early history, as described by the prophets, nets startling conclusions.

So goes a little, an introduction, of my circumspect *opinions* on the realities and implications of archeological evidences integrated into the scriptural history of Adam and the patriarchs. Selah. *Ddd* :o)

Bibliography

DHC and HC: [Documentary] *History of the Church of Jesus Christ of Latter-day Saints*, Deseret Book Company, 1970, 1973 Reprint.

Four Standard Works comprises The Holy Bible, The Book of Mormon, The Doctrine and Covenants, and The Pearl of Great Price of the Church of Jesus Christ of Latter-day Saints. Note: also contained therein are the Topical Guide, the Bible Dictionary, the Joseph Smith Translation, and other reference materials.

FWP, Elder Alvin R Dyer, *For What Purpose,* talk given in Oslo, Norway, 18Mar1962. Original transcript in LDS Church Archives.

JR1. Dennis D Doddridge, *Journal of References Vol. 1, the Adam-God Revelation*, DD Enterprises, Allyn, WA, 1977, 2012, Updated 12/21/15.

YOUNG, Brigham. President Brigham and other Church leaders. *Journal of Discourses.* 26 volumes. Brigham Young University Library. Salt Lake City, UT. Photo Lithographic Reprint of Exact Original Edition: Reprint 1964. No.34271.

ST. JOSEPH "NEW CATHOLIC EDITION" OF THE HOLY BIBLE. Catholic Book Publishing Company, New York, 1962. (Abbreviated herein as NCE)

SEER, THE, Orson Pratt, *The Seer, Jan. 1853-Aug. 1854, a bound collection of periodicals, epistles, etc.,* printed and published in Washington DC and in Liverpool, England by Orson Pratt and Franklin D Richards.

SMITH Jr., Joseph *The Holy Scriptures Translated and Corrected by the Spirit of Revelation by Joseph Smith, Jr. The Seer,* The Church of Jesus Christ of Latter-day Saints, Robert Smith, I.L. Rogers, E. Robinson, Publishing Committee, 1867.

SMITH Jr., Joseph, *The Holy Scriptures Containing the Old and New Testaments, An Inspired Version of the Authorized Version – A New Corrected Edition*, The Reorganized Church of Jesus Christ of Latter-Day Saints, Herald Publishing House, Independence, Missouri, Thirteenth Printing, June 1967.

USSHER James, Archbishop of Armagh Church of Ireland, *The Annals of the World*, Printed by E. Tyler, for F. Crook and G. Bedell, London, 1658. (Note: various pdf copies were reviewed. The primary pdf copy used in this book is from *Bennie Blount Ministries International.org. their website stating, "Copy Freely." May 2018.* Hard copy was also compared; also see *https://archive.org/details/AnnalsOfTheWorld*, May 2018.)

YAC, Robert Young, *Young's Analytical Concordance to the Bible*, Wm B Eerdmans Publishing Co., Grand Rapids, MI, Reprinted 1977.

Charts, Graphs, and Pictures

Glossary

Annals. Short for Annals of the World by James Ussher.

Arphaxad-Nahor Seven. A term by the author for the second group of Patriarchs, comprising seven Patriarchs (after the first group of 11). This second had much shorter longevities than the first 11 and had what the author regards as a more normal age for having their firstborn sons, 33.0 years for the first three of the seven, and 30.25 year average for the next four of the seven patriarchs. The combined average for the seven is 31.4 years. See p29.

Birth-age, Birth-year. See explanation in Notes.

Composition and Decomposition. A doctrine taught by Brigham Young that every particle in the universe is either composing (organizing) to ever greater heights of perfection or decomposing back into native element.

> My simple philosophy is this. The elements of which this terra firma is composed, are every moment either composing or decomposing. They commence to organize or to compose, and continue to grow until they arrive at their zenith of perfection, and then they begin to decompose. *(Brigham Young, Oct 09, 1852, JD1:219)*

For more information on this topic, please consider the book "Composition, Decomposition, and Eternity" by Dennis D Doddridge, available in hard copy and eKindle.

Evolutionize. A term I employ to denote the process of evolution developing beings and animals without organized spirits to the point of compatibility with beings and animals who do have organized spirits. These beings are then useful by introducing immortals to the physical infirmities of mortality.

It should be noted here that a goodly number of general authorities of the Church of Jesus Christ of Latter-day Saints have over the years expressed alternate ideologies opposing evolution and related topics.

First Flesh. A term which refers solely to life with souls. Adam was the first life *with a soul* upon the earth, hence he was the *first flesh* with a soul on the earth. See p.166.

Generation. There are a number of definitions for the word *generation*, both biblical and contemporary. As used in this book *by the author* the length of a generation is from *the birth of one father until the birth of his firstborn son*. The word is also used elsewhere in this book in quotations and those definitions are set by the person being quoted.

Intelligence. (1) While the terms "intelligence" and "intelligent" denote the ability to learn and use knowledge and apply expertise, something all life has to a greater or lesser degree, (2) "intelligence" also denotes a form of spirit matter, one of the two highest forms in existence, the other being the Holy Spirit. Intelligences, through agency, seek to become *organized* gods. The Holy Spirit provides their means to achieve this goal through "eternal progression." Intelligences are either male or female, whereas the Holy Spirit has no gender.

Mortal Existence. The period of time that we each as mortals spend here on earth. Collectively, the mortal existence of mankind comprises the first 6,000 years of the 7,000-year temporal existence, the balance being the Millennium.

Mortalization. Transitioning from immortality to mortality took centuries as the blood in the Patriarchs' veins became more dominant by continually eating mortal foods, instead of spiritual vegetation their first parents ate in the Garden. The *spirit fluid* in their veins gradually accommodated the blood. At first the Patriarchs waited 65-187 years, all the while consuming mortal foods, before having their firstborn child in order to reduce their overall longevities down to 120 years (see p.21). It went slowly. But Noah waited nearly 500 years. This then expedited the desired effect to reduce the longevity of mortals down to the goal of 120 years.

Organized spirit. All tangible physical matter in the universe can be labelled as *physical* or *spirit* (technically, spirit matter is also tangible). Primordially, both physical and spirit matters are known as "native elements," wholly unorganized. Gods may organize unorganized spirit matter *through procreation* with their wives, the same as we do with physical matter. As mortals we ingest temporarily organized physical matter in the form of food. Through procreation the result is organized mortal children. Gods likewise ingest spirit foods. Through procreation the result is organized spirit children. Furthermore, each of us, as spirit children was synthesized, while still in the resurrected mother's womb, with *an eternal individual intelligence*. We *are* those eternal individual intelligences *(D&C 93:29)*. Similarly, spirit animals procreate spirit offspring, though they do not possess godlike intelligences. Not all mortal lifeforms have counterpart organized spirits.

Patriarchal son. The son who becomes the lineal patriarch of the family, normally, but not always, the firstborn son.

Pre-Adamites. Evolutionized beings who lived before, during and after Adam.

Selah. An ancient Hebraic word in the Bible with no known definition. I use it here to culminate this book, to mean "So it is."

Soul. D&C 88:15 "And the spirit and the body are the soul of man."

Spirit. (1) A refined form of uncreated intelligent matter, universally found in a scale of a myriad of levels, from godlike to demonic. While demonic spirit matter and demons possess no intelligence, they are nevertheless quite intelligent in their efforts to decompose all existence.

It may well be that unorganized *mortal* matter is but a heavy, low-level, but composable form of spirit matter not found in the eternal worlds. When resurrected, it will play a crucial role in the eternal progression of all life.

> 7 There is no such thing as immaterial matter. All spirit is matter, but it is more fine or pure, and can only be discerned by purer eyes;
>
> 8 We cannot see it; but when our bodies are purified we shall see that it is all matter. *(D&C 131:7, 8)*

(2) Short for "organized spirit."

(3) "Spirit fluid" is spirit element that flows in the veins of immortals instead of blood. Even in mortality, our immortal spirits must still retain spirit fluid in our spirit veins. Blood will not sustain our spirits. Furthermore, we would otherwise need a speedy spirit fluid transfusion upon our mortal deaths.

Temporal Existence. "As there is one day out of seven set apart, sanctified and ordained as a day of rest, so there is one thousand years set apart as a day of rest **out of the seven thousand which will constitute the temporal existence** of our earth. That will be the time when the Lord Jesus will reign as King of kings and Lord of lords." *(Orson Pratt, JD 14:351; ba)*

Young Earth. "Young Earth creationism is a form of creationism, a religious belief, which holds that the universe, Earth, and all life on Earth were created by direct acts of God less than 10,000 years ago." *(Wikipedia, Young Earth creationism;[viewed 02Jun15] see also p.9)*

Index

Notes

1. Many of the scriptures included herein contain particular parts worth putting into **bold print**. Rather than type at the end of each (bold font added) to indicate that the bold font was not in the original, a simple *"(ba)"* is added at the end.

2. Certain Scriptures are given **added clarity** by the insertion of a locution, placed in smaller font in brackets, as for example: ***[day and hour].*** At the end of the quote, a *[ ]* is added to indicate this insert.

3. **Abbreviations used in this book**

AD. Anno Domini (in the year of the Lord). Use to represent years starting with the birth of Christ and forward.

AM. Anno Mundi, a Jewish chronology calendar.

BC. Before Christ.

D&C. *The Doctrine and Covenants of the Church of Jesus Christ of Latter-day Saints.*

Ddd. Dennis D Doddridge.

JD. *Journal of Discourses.*

JP. Julian Period. Created by a French scholar, Joseph Justus Scaliger (1540-1609), who applied only positive numbers to a chronological system comprised of 7980 years, rather than applying BC and AD.

JR1. *Journal of References, Volume 1. (See Bibliography.)*

JST. Joseph Smith Translation of the Bible (Inspired Version).

KJV. King James Version of the Bible.

LDS. Refers to [The Church of Jesus Christ of] **L**atter-**d**ay **S**aints used in some references in this book such as *lds.org. With reference to the Church or its members the term "LDS" is now obsolete.*

Note: Several Internet sources were also researched, compared and utilized.

NCE. St. Joseph New Catholic Edition of the Holy Bible.

PDF. Portable Document Format is a file format.

➢ Regarding the use of asterisks in this book, sometimes putting the reason for the asterisk close to the thought being expanded rather than later as a footnote saves space and one does not need to jump around to read the supportive reference material. Asterisks in the Ussher Chronology Excerpts sections are not mine but refer to Ussher's own myriad sources. Exceptions: *Ddd notes* on various pages.

➢ Other scriptural verses include those found in *The Pearl of Great Price, The Doctrine and Covenants,* and *The Book of Mormon,* all published by the Church of Jesus Christ of Latter-day Saints.

➢ Rather than write "the age of the father when his direct line or firstborn son was born" each time I refer to that thought, I have written simply **"birth-age,"** or **"birth-year."**

SCRIPTURAL REFERENCES BY PAGE

This book contains a number of scriptures which are only referred to, but the full quote is not given. This section provides those quotes, for the benefit of the reader not having immediate access to the Scriptures. References by Ussher are quite numerous and are not added in this section.

All scriptures quoted in this book, unless otherwise indicated, are per **the Four Standard Works** of the Church of Jesus Christ of Latter-day Saints.

P.23 D&C 20:26 Not only those who believed after he came in the meridian of time, in the flesh,...; **D&C 39:3** The same which came in the meridian of time unto mine own, and mine own received me not; **Moses 5:57** For they would not hearken unto his voice, nor believe on his Only Begotten Son, even him whom he declared should come in the meridian of time, who was prepared from before the foundation of the world.; **Moses 6:57** ... Jesus Christ, a righteous Judge, who shall come in the meridian of time.; **Moses 6:62 ...** through the blood of mine Only Begotten, who shall come in the meridian of time.; **Moses 7:45,46** ... When shall the blood of the Righteous be shed, that all they that mourn may be sanctified and have eternal life? 46 And the Lord said: It shall be in the meridian of time, ...

P.32 & 63 Matt. 24:21, 22

21 For then shall be great tribulation, such as was not since the beginning of the world to this time, no, nor ever shall be.

22 And except those days should be shortened, there should no flesh be saved: but for the elect's sake those days shall be shortened.

P.48 1 Chron. 1:1,2

1 Adam, Sheth, Enosh, 2 Kenan, Mahalaleel, Jered,

P.51 Exo.18:12

And Jethro, Moses' father in law, took a burnt offering and sacrifices for God: and Aaron came, and all the elders of Israel, to eat bread with Moses' father in law before God.

P.77 Acts 17:26

And hath made of one blood all nations of men for to dwell on all the face of the earth, and hath determined the times before appointed, and the bounds of their habitation;

P.77 D&C 124:49

Verily, verily, I say unto you, that when I give a commandment to any of the sons of men to do a work unto my name, and those sons of men go with all their might and with all they have to perform that work, and cease not their diligence, and their enemies come upon them and hinder them from performing that work, behold, it behooveth me to require that work no more at the hands of those sons of men, but to accept of their offerings.

P.84 D&C 88:110-116

110 ... Satan shall be bound, that old serpent, who is called the devil, and shall not be loosed for the space of a thousand years.

111 And then he shall be loosed for a little season, that he may gather together his armies.

112 And Michael, the seventh angel, even the archangel, shall gather together his armies, even the hosts of heaven.

113 And the devil shall gather together his armies; even the hosts of hell, and shall come up to battle against Michael and his armies.

114 And then cometh the battle of the great God; and the devil and his armies shall be cast away into their own place, that they shall not have power over the saints any more at all. ...

P.86 *Additional reference to Adam's creation subject on pp.86-88, 166.*

Man began life as a human being, in the likeness of our heavenly Father. True it is that the body of man enters upon its career as a tiny germ embryo, which becomes an infant, quickened at a certain stage by the spirit whose tabernacle it is, and the child, after being born, develops into a man. There is nothing in this, however, to indicate that the original man, the first of our race, began life as anything less than a man, or less than the human germ or embryo that becomes a man. *(Excerpts from a statement by the First Presidency of the Church, Dec 18, 1909, From "Messages of the First Presidency," Vol. 4 pp 200-207, (also Deseret News, Dec 18, 1909). The Origins of Man. Signed, Joseph F. Smith, John R. Winder, Anthon H. Lund, First Presidency of the Church of Jesus Christ of Latter-day Saints.)*

P.165 2 Pet. 3:10-13

10 But the day of the Lord will come as a thief in the night; in the which the heavens shall pass away with a great noise, and the elements shall melt with fervent heat, the earth also and the works that are therein shall be burned up.

11 *Seeing* then *that* all these things shall be dissolved, what manner *of persons* ought ye to be in *all* holy conversation and godliness,

12 Looking for and hasting unto the coming of the day of God, wherein the heavens being on fire shall be dissolved, and the elements shall melt with fervent heat?

13 Nevertheless we, according to his promise, look for new heavens and a new earth, wherein dwelleth righteousness.

P.170 Alma 5:14

And now behold, I ask of you, my brethren of the church, have ye spiritually been born of God? Have ye received his image in your countenances? Have ye experienced this mighty change in your hearts?

P.174 Joshua 24:2

And Joshua said unto all the people, Thus saith the LORD God of Israel, Your fathers dwelt on the other side of the flood in old time, *even* Terah, the father of Abraham, and the father of Nachor: and they served other gods.

P.178 Ether 2:3

And they did also carry with them deseret, which, by interpretation, is a honey bee; and thus they did carry with them swarms of bees, and all manner of that which was upon the face of the land, seeds of every kind.

P.184 D&C 93:29

Man was also in the beginning with God. Intelligence, or the light of truth, was not created or made, neither indeed can be.

Grace After Works

By Dennis D Doddridge

Starting with the Bible and using latter-day verse to clarify and strengthen the Biblical teachings upon the subjects of grace and works, this effort endeavors to provide the reader with a fresh and independent look at the relationship of Grace to Works.